Coming Alive

Coming Alive

Anne Ierardi

MEMOIR

SHANTI ARTS PUBLISHING
BRUNSWICK, MAINE

Coming Alive: Memoir

Published by Shanti Arts Publishing

Cover and interior design by Shanti Arts Designs

Shanti Arts LLC
Brunswick, Maine

www.shantiarts.com

Printed in the United States of America

This book is a memoir, written from the author's recollections of experiences that occurred over many years. The dialogue presented in this book is not intended to represent word-for-word transcripts; events and scenes are not precise representations. The names and characteristics of some individuals have been changed to protect privacy. In all cases, the author has remained true to the feeling and meaning of what happened and what was said.

ISBN: 978-1-956056-19-8 (softcover)
ISBN: 978-1-956056-25-9 (ebook)

Library of Congress Control Number: 2021952934

To Judy
il mio cuore è sempre tuo

Contents

Acknowledgements 9

Prologue 13

The Announcement 15

Leaving Home

California, Here I Come 21
Beautiful Mind 30
Hollywood, Lovers, and other Strangers 33
Energy vs. Repression 37
Italy 40
Sister Wisdom 43
The Moon, My Mother, and Me 48
Consolation 53

Coming Out
The First Call: 1975–82

Half In and Half Out 59
Italian Lesbians 63
The Italian Mouse 66
Laurie's Party 68
Cappuccino's 72
The Ultimatum 73

Healing and the Church
The Second Call: 1982–84

Healthsigns 79
Catholic Meets Protestant 82
Sorrows Past and Present 87
Across the Charles 91
Les Jolies Roses 93

Gay Rites
The Third Call: 1984–88

Chapel Week: Fall 99

Chrysalis: Winter 101
Preaching as Divine Activity: Spring 104
Gay Rites: Summer 106
Revolutionary Integrity 108
Worcester 110
The Heidi House 118
Walden 120

Ordination
The Fourth Call: 1988–90

Leaving Boston for New England 127
Italian Protestant 129
Telling the Truth in Love 132
Living the Gospel 135

A Selection of Anne Ierardi's Paintings 140

Cape Cod Artist
The Fifth Call: 1990–2005

On Cape Cod 151
Abide with Me 157
L-Shaped House 163
Dr. Duchy 167
Icons 172
Crossing the Bridge 174

Legal Marriage
The Sixth Call: 2005

Wedding Bells 181
Letting Go 186
Redemption Songs 190
Stalking the Gaps at Low Tide 193

Author's Notes about Sources 197

About the Author 199

Acknowledgments

TWO DECADES OF EFFORT AND INSPIRATION HAVE GONE INTO MAKING THIS book. Many more decades formed me as the person in the memoir. As a child, my Aunt Portia, a language professor whom the family said I most resembled, sent me books about female heroines. Later, I sought out fairy tales, mysteries, biographies, and novels. Above all, it's the people and communities in this memoir who made a difference in my life.

Grazie mille to my grandparents, who càme here at the turn of the twentieth century, passing on a living tradition filled with humor, *una tavola italiana*, through good times and bad. My parents, John and Theresa; stepfather, Tony; brothers, Johnny and Anthony; my nieces, nephews, aunts, uncles, cousins, all my extended family.

The process of getting a book published depends on many people and organizations, including editors, publicists, media helpers, and authors.

Diane O'Connell, developmental editor, raised the bar to reveal my own voice in the memoir. "Truth telling" is the obstacle to overcome as she gently and with humor got me to go deeper. Carol McManus, for opening the world of social media and guiding me this past year with unfailing positivity. Deep appreciation to my publisher, Christine Cote of Shanti Arts, for her vision bringing art together with the written word and her ability, patience, and collaboration in shaping this memoir into its beautiful form.

Thank you to the Author's Guild, the Blue Hills Summer Memoir Institute, the Fine Arts Work Center, David Groff, Brian Jud, Gillian Lancaster, Peter Murphy, Caridad Pineiro, Olga Vezeris, and Erin White.

Special thanks to the many listeners, readers, and encouragers: Ann Boover, Margaret Murphy, Cindy Maybeck and Elaine Faden, Jane O'Hara Shields, Ellen Chahey, Louise DeSantis Deutsch, Susan Scribner, Margaret Nichol, Pavia, Rita Sherwin, Frank and Jane Recknagel, Sylvia Karkus Furash. Ann Michele Rogers-Brigham, Marcia West, Joel Chaison, Monica Styron, Paula Feinstein and Marilyn Greenberg, Les Pappas, Peg Schultz-Akerson, Jo-an Stone, Virginia Furtwangler, Victoria Miller.

Patricia Papernow, for walking with me all those years, her editing skills, most of all for her open heart. Barbara Smith-Moran, for her spirited friendship. Mary Hunt, for her careful reading and understanding of my woman's soul journey. For Robert Fox, teacher, supervisor, mentor, and long-time existential visionary brother.

The International Women Writers Guild (IWWG) has continued to impart wisdom through women's empowerment. Special thanks to Susan Tiberghien for her inspired teaching and soulful memoirs, and Dorothy Randall Gray for bringing "dance and joy" birthing creative expression.

At IWWG, I met "mentor to be" Kathleen Spivack, whose workshops and love of Cape Cod began our enduring friendship. Kathleen sparked the fire in me and built a foundation for belief in myself as an author. She brought together writers and artists on the Cape to hone our craft and offer readings with Sharon and Milton at the Teichmann Gallery.

After I moved to Cape Cod, I soon met Marion Vuilleumier, trailblazer and founder of the Cape Cod Writer's Center. Through the dedicated leadership of Nancy Rubin Stuart and Barbara Eppich Struna, Marion's vision lives on. For five years I thrived through a memoir writers group. Special thanks to Andrew Singer and Katrina Valenzuela for their shared wisdom and reading, and to Priscilla McCormick who kept cheering me on, never tiring of reading my manuscript and offering solid ideas.

Having good friends like Ellen Chahey and Ed Maroney can lead to almost anything! Ed called me one day and asked if I would fill in and do a write-up on an open mic at a church, and by the way, "bring your guitar." For the next five years, I interviewed musicians and wrote a column for the *Barnstable Patriot*.

My passion for preaching and the ethics that informed good writing were a gift to me by the late Rev. Dr. Katie Geneva Cannon. I am grateful the Katie G. Cannon Womanist Center in Richmond is carrying on her "work that the soul must have."

For over forty years, the Healthsigns Board and Friends have brought forward with love and joy many gatherings of art, music, healing, ecumenical partnerships, and a coalition of welcoming (LGBTQ) congregations. I have been blessed with many inspiring colleagues in ministry. Special appreciation to the New England Women Minister's Association for thirty years of loving sisterhood and annual retreats at Miramar Retreat Center in Duxbury.

Artists abound in this rich soil of Cape Cod. My painting flourished in Provincetown and Castle Hill Center for the Arts in Truro with Salvatore Del Deo, John Grillo, Cynthia Packard, Suzanne Packer, and Leslie Jackson.

During quarantine, I was grateful for more time to paint and write. Special appreciation for all my Zoom and Blog friends including Mes Amies, Healthsigns groups, and my cherished Friday group: Annie, Sue, Don, Marilyn, Judy, Mike, Bill.

To Judy for forty-two years of sharing, our mutual vocations of healing body, mind, and spirit, and countless hours of revisions.

For Duchy, mini poodle from Poodle Rescue of New England, who lay beside me for eighteen years in the writing of this book.

For Dolce, toy poodle from Poodle Rescue of Connecticut, who is fast becoming "our dog."

Anne Ierardi
Cape Cod, Massachusetts

Roman Chalice

Prologue

WHAT DOES IT MEAN TO COME ALIVE? TO LET THE PAST UNRAVEL ITS CLAIMS, confusions, and containers? To let my feet take me on the road to find out?

My thirst to know God came naturally to me, as it did for my fellow New England traveler:

> I never spoke with God,
> Nor visited in heaven;
> Yet certain am I of the spot
> As if the chart were given.
>
> —Emily Dickinson

To be alive is to come alive. Hearing the call and accepting the invitation. Coming out again and again, engaging with the world. My road led to a theology of relatedness, the I and Thou.

My life has evolved over the past fifty years. I now feel the hands of Divine Providence lifting up beauty, touching soul-to-soul, making meaning out of despair, offering peace in turbulent times. Learning to paint opened my eyes to see and my soul to express visually without words.

That was good, very good, but it wasn't enough.

Counselors, teachers, mentors, friends embodied the spirit of Christ to me in their words, actions, and prayers. To be a "good Catholic," I had to let go, make a new beginning to become whole in my body and to celebrate the precious gift God gave me: life as a woman; life as a gay woman.

That was good, very good, but God knew it still wasn't enough.

"You will be a pastor, a counselor. I call you to make a way in the wilderness. I will introduce you to a physician at an astrology party. Together you will birth a holistic center to minister to other seekers of all faiths and backgrounds. Through the ebb and flow of community, you will learn wisdom, celebrate beauty, and live happily by the sea."

"I am afraid, Lord. I am not enough."

"You are an artist. There is more to come; for I have come that you may have life and have it to the full."

ONE

The Announcement

NOVEMBER ARRIVED, A BITTER MONTH. SUNDAY MORNING AFTER THE service, five sets of eyes stared at me, looking tense as they huddled in the senior pastor's office. Why would they call an impromptu pastoral relations meeting after church, I wondered? The usual small talk may have occurred as it does when people are uncomfortable and about to drop a bombshell, yet all I remember is looking to the chairperson as my heart started pounding. Elea sat upright right next to me, eyes downcast, as she nervously read from a sheet of paper: "We have decided to abolish the position of Associate Pastor as we need to utilize the money for a new furnace. We do not plan to hire another Associate Pastor."

Elea was a Baptist elder whom I had trusted over the past two years to help me adjust to the parish and rural town. I ministered to her when her husband was dying. The previous spring on the night before Easter, I had slept over at Elea's house so I could be there for the sunrise service to play "Morning Has Broken" on my guitar. The sweet smell of Elea's cardamom bread—a Finnish specialty—wafted into the guest room that morning. I couldn't square my perception of this strong Christian woman with the person now making this pronouncement. And where was the Senior Pastor?

Though shocked, I remained in character, hiding my emotions as I walked out of the room, stunned. I couldn't wait to get out of the room that seemed to be closing in on me. I sat down at my desk. My office, a makeshift space partitioned on two sides with no privacy for a phone conversation, was situated in a larger room with a conference-size table and metal chairs. Within a few minutes after I left the meeting, Pastor Ned's sheepish face peaked over the side of my cubicle to see how I was doing. His ruby-red round face magnified concern and sympathy while his body shifted and his eyes looked away from me. His stance seemed to be saying, "I just couldn't help what happened!"

I had come to see how the male dominance in ministry in the seventies and eighties had sunk many a hopeful ship of seminary-trained women desiring only to serve their congregations and give generously of their gifts. Many Christian "nice guys" were threatened by women entering their domain.

Still, my spirit was open and free as I had just returned from a clergywoman's retreat and been made to feel more hopeful and affirmative than on previous retreats during which women cried and raged about the disrespect and abuses they had encountered in their early parish work.

Replaced by a furnace. Jesus Jones!—an expression I picked up from my southern girlfriend. Is this church? Is this what pastors meant by "clergy killers?" Instead, I felt the pathos of Holy Week. The crucifixion began with his disciples, those guys Jesus trusted. The cock crowed thrice. Not once, but three times. When I watched filmstrips of this scene in my childhood catechism class, I felt Jesus's disappointment with Peter in my heart. How could I bear this betrayal? How could I face my congregation?

As it turned out, Ned left me that afternoon to mind the church as he was leaving for his favorite retreat: a hunting expedition. Now that he had committed his cowardly deed, he was ready for an unsuspecting deer.

Betrayed and angry, I sped home, crossing the bridge to the safety of Cape Cod where I had settled when this job took me south of my native home of Boston. What could I do now? Why hadn't I left right after I received my doctorate that was hardly acknowledged by the pastor? Should I politely speak to other church leaders to understand why this happened or was it time for confrontation? Who had hatched my dismissal outside of the usual procedures? Was there a high road?

In retrospect, there was one clue I could not decipher. As I recalled, the pastoral relations committee had met with me at some point that year, saying they wanted me to be more visible. "What did they mean?" I wondered to myself, frustrated. I was a part-time minister, but I drove forty-five miles to the church as often as possible. Yes, I was there physically, and yes, I did my best to care for them pastorally. Yet I didn't feel safe there. I didn't really know who my allies were. How could I be me? I could not come out without losing my position. I was different in so many ways: educated, urban, feminist, Catholic turned Baptist, and gay.

Invisible. A lonely place feeling oddly familiar.

The next Sunday I was to preach while Ned was away. In my new home on Cape Cod, I sat at my desk overlooking our large oak tree, asking God for strength and guidance as I formulated how I might speak the truth in love.

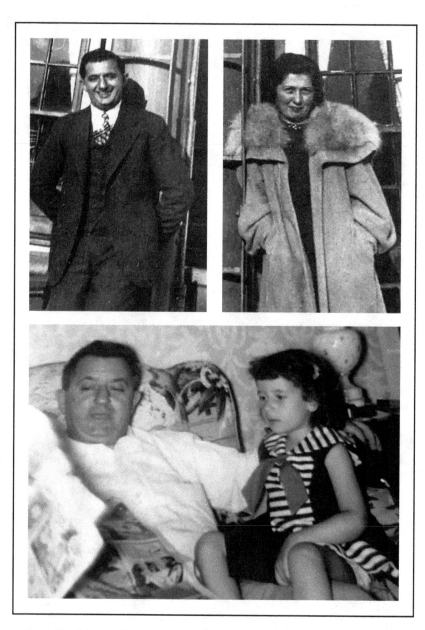

[top] My father and mother on their honeymoon [bottom] Daddy reading me the funny pages

Leaving Home

I realized my life was not only shaped by my thoughts, but by the places that connected me to my heart; that made me "come alive."

[top left] My grandparents: Anthony Ierardi and Anna Rosa Allegretti Ierardi; and Joseph Verrochi and Concetta Marinucci Verrochi [top right] Aunty Portia, Anna, and Rosie "Angel" [bottom left] On the road to Capri [bottom right] Freshman year

TWO

California, Here I Come

Anxiety is the dizziness of freedom.

—Soren Kierkegaard

FREEDOM BECKONED ME TO VENTURA COUNTY. IT WAS 1970. SINGING along with Cat Stevens, I too was "on the road to find out." Southern California—so different from my home in Boston. The sun dried my skin. I missed the crispness of fall, bright colors saturating the landscape. As one of my roommates quipped when I invited her to visit me in Boston: "I can't go east because the sun rises on the wrong side of the ocean."

California Lutheran College was small, in its infancy, surrounded by hills on one side and track housing on the other. As soon as I opened my mouth, my new California friends gleefully noticed my distinct Bostonian manner of speaking: "tonic" for pop or soda, and "jimmies" on ice cream.

I couldn't stomach the food in the cafeteria, and I didn't eat for three weeks. To me, food was Italian-American food prepared by my mother, who catered to me with special dishes. My mother shone in the kitchen, the most loving room in our house. It was there I sat doing my homework when I came home from school while she cooked dinner. How could I ever survive in a fluorescent-lit cafeteria?

One day in an advanced philosophy class, our professor, speaking of the theories of Anglican bishop George Berkeley, held up a chair to show that it did not exist, proving the limitations of materialism. In other words, the chair exists only because of our mind's ability to perceive it. I didn't get that at all! As he lifted high the chair, I felt a queasy feeling in my gut and wondered if I too might not exist.

So many changes occurred in my family in the years following my father's death. At seventeen, I didn't know what I would find, but I knew I had to leave home. I could not have gone out west if my older brother Johnny hadn't first ventured to Los Angeles in his late twenties to work for United Artists in their newly created international cassette tape department. I missed him more than I realized. He called home every week, directing me to the best movies and musicals in Boston. When *Mame* came to the Shubert Theatre, he told my mother to write a note to get me out of high school early so I could make the matinee. There in the first row of the first balcony, Angela Lansbury filled me up and encouraged me to reach upwards and "open a new window!"

Johnny felt the weight of responsibility after my father died suddenly of a heart attack. He helped my mother financially until she found work as a lab assistant at Harvard Medical School. He set our social and entertainment agenda. He bought his first convertible in his early twenties, and later, my brother Anthony followed suit and got his own dark blue Mercury convertible. Anthony, four years younger than Johnny, nicknamed him "the King," while Johnny called him "my Anthony" because my mother often referred to him in this special way: "Just look at the flowers my Anthony brought me."

A typical outing with Johnny at the helm began with dinner at Olympia, a Greek restaurant in Boston, then passes to a premier showing of *The Sound of Music.* Just as the Rolling Stones were becoming famous, Johnny surprised me with three tickets to see their concert in Worcester. He made a big deal of having to drive me and my cousin Carolyn to listen to that loud nonmelodic music. In Johnny's characteristic way, he quietly charmed a friend from London Records to get us backstage to the dressing room to meet the Stones.

The room was large and bare. There they were: Mick Jagger holding a Coke bottle even larger than his face; Keith Richards—or was it Charlie Watts—pulling the bottom wire of coat hangers on a long rack; and Brian Jones hiding under a mop of blonde, almost white, hair, quietly embracing his guitar as he fingered the neck soundlessly. I was led around to each Stone so they might autograph my large program book. How grand to be led into the lion's den (isn't Mick a Leo?) of the world of British rockers.

When I turned eleven, Johnny came home with my first guitar and paid for weekly lessons after he saw me in the basement strumming my mother's mop pole with a piece of rope for the strap. Every Wednesday after school, I carried my dark brown Harmony guitar on the crowded MBTA buses and walked half a mile to Bob Mulcahy's home. His studio was in the third-floor attic. The low-ceilinged room had black and white photographs of my beloved teacher's career: Bob conducting the children's orchestra, probably from the fifties; in the forties, there was Bob playing jazz guitar in the Dean Martin and Jerry Lewis Band. After a young boy hurried out of the studio with his electric guitar, Bob would appear, annunciating my name the correct European way: "Miss Ierardi."

Bob called me his rock-and-roll expert. One day he showed me a fake book of rock tunes and asked me to pick out the best ones, quoting Duke Ellington: "There are only two kinds of music: good music and the other kind." Bob transposed many songs for the guitar—popular and old standards. I learned the music of the thirties through the sixties. However, my fantasy of being in a pop band never materialized. I was a girl in the era of boy bands.

On Sundays Johnny drove Anthony and me to church while my mother cooked Sunday dinner at home. For us, the loving preparation of food for the family was as sacred and essential as attending Mass. Johnny chose a different Catholic church than the one the Archdiocese of Boston assigned us because St. Susannah's was modern and open to change. It was the beginning of the changes brought by the Second Vatican Council, and suddenly, we began to sing hymns. Anthony and I joked that Johnny was never late for a movie, only for church. We thought no one knew us there, as the Catholic churches were packed with parishioners and seemed impersonal. Later we learned we did not go unnoticed. On his honeymoon in Bermuda, Anthony met a couple who recognized him as part of the family "who came in late" at St. Susannah's.

Johnny loved inviting his diverse mixture of friends and co-workers home for dinner to delight in my mother's Italian meals and meet our family. He enjoyed going out to piano bars in Boston, often to hear his friend Ellen White play at the Lenox Hotel. As my mother was getting ready for bed, Johnny would be pressing his pants in the kitchen and getting dressed to go out. She worried about him and "the other jerks on the road at night." Johnny would distract her by playfully repeating her saying, "Go out one night and stay in the next!"

I was one of only two students in my neighborhood high school who left Massachusetts for college. My mother had a surprise party for me with my high school friends. I packed a huge black trunk and took the train out to Los Angeles. At the station, my mother cried, and my stepfather felt he was losing the family he had grown to love. He begged, "Anne, don't leave me with your mother."

Memories came on the long train ride to Los Angeles and wonderings about what was ahead. I had "developed early," a euphemism of the times for growing breasts sooner than others. I don't remember how it happened, but one day I was flat, and the next, two large balls of flesh appeared on my tiny chest. My mother had a secret agenda and planned a weekend with my cousin Carolyn. "Tell Anne the facts of life and get her to stop wearing an undershirt."

Cousin Carolyn was the daughter of my mother's oldest brother, whom they called Big Mike (in contrast to Aunty Lena's husband, Mike, who was short). Carolyn grew up fast in a household of adults. She was only a few years older than me, but when you are young, the gap seems enormous. The family gossip machine spewed out shock when Carolyn wore make-up or attended mature musicals—like *Gypsy*!

Carolyn had a way with words; they rolled off her tongue like Barbra Streisand in *Funny Girl*. Carolyn was the star of her show. My brothers and I loved visiting her family, especially at their beach house in Scituate across from the harbor.

At age eleven I was thrilled to have a weekend with sixteen-year-old Carolyn in her stucco brown mansion, until her words took on a serious, hesitant manner about changes that take place in a young girl's life. She said her daddy, "Big Mike," was excited and proud when those changes in puberty became official, but I couldn't fathom that. Even though my father was dead, I could not imagine him receiving such news with excitement in the presence of my mother.

Later, in Carolyn's bedroom, she pulled out a box like the one my mother kept in her closet. "Napkins," my mother had said. Strange that a meticulous housekeeper like my mother would store napkins in her clothes closet! Now Carolyn was pulling these napkins out of the box and telling me they went on my body. All I could imagine was they went somewhere between my breasts and my underarm. Carolyn assured me that I didn't need them now. All I wanted was to have her finish her adult talk and get back to being *Funny Girl*.

❊

As I looked out the train window, seeing the moon shining over the cactus in Arizona, my reverie took me back to high school. It was the last day before graduation. I crossed the teacher's picket line to say goodbye to Miss Ward. Her last words to me were: "I hope you don't mind that I kept your portrait of your classmate on the wall of my kitchen."

Did I mind that Miss Ward kept my drawing? I was thrilled, amazed, awed that my pastel work was hanging in her kitchen! I remembered the day in class when she asked for volunteers to model, after having explained how to get Caucasian skin color in our pastel drawings. A tall, brown-skinned girl, shyly raised her hand from the back of the first row. Miss Ward smiled and said, "Forget what I just told you." Intense color and strong warm features expressed what I beheld in this strikingly beautiful classmate of mine.

Miss Ward wore round, wire-rimmed glasses like a "hip" sixties person—a cross between Mia Farrow and the Beatles in their colorful *Sgt. Pepper's Lonely Hearts Club Band* days. She appeared unlike our other teachers, who, though kindly, were typical relics of the Boston school system. Mr. Napoleon Fontaine, our French teacher, resembled Jiminy Cricket. Affectionately, he tapped me on the head with his pencil as we translated the wonderfully humorous stories of Alphonse Daudet and Guy De Maupassant.

I stood at Miss Ward's side at her desk while she opened a huge art book. The painting she showed me was full of life and color. The woman had a line of green-yellow pigment on her nose; her dress was bright orange with green trim; and her black and purple hair was formed into a bun. Later, I knew it was Madame Matisse painted by her husband, the great Post-Impressionist artist. This was my first glimpse into the tradition I would come to express naturally in my paintings.

Besides my love of the art room, I also came alive in English classes. Sophomore year my class was located in the basement of the ochre-yellow brick school in a wing off the cafeteria. Rounding the corner of the corridor, I knew I'd find her observing all her students as we made our way into her class. She had that "Miss Marple" look, as if she knew something you didn't. Mrs. O'Neil was waiting for me. She had light blue eyes, white hair, and a grand Irish twinkle just like my godmother. She didn't stand in the dark corridor as other teachers did to police us. Her eyes were lit up with humor, mischief, and wisdom. She saw me, the one who hid, and knew I was secretly yearning to be seen by her. One day she came over and repositioned me: "Walk with your head in the air, not down on the floor." Any embarrassment I might have felt was softened by her firm but winsome personality.

Mrs. O'Neil believed in causes, my first real introduction to social justice. It was unusual in 1967 in the Boston schools to have a cause. While the rest of the nation was in the midst of the civil rights movement and changing values, we were kept ignorant. The one significant victory happened when a group of girls came to school dressed in slacks. They were sent home, but they marched to the office of the school committee in downtown Boston. From that day on, girls could wear pants to school.

Mrs. O'Neil wrote on the blackboard the words "Cesar Chavez." She told us of the poor conditions of migrant farmers and how Chavez did something about it. I wanted to know more. When a tall, lanky boy in class named Gerard teased her by asking her a question about the meaning of a word, she cajoled him: "Get out your dictionary and look it up. I will give you five points just to look it up." She was always giving us points that made up our grade. Grades were given based on initiative and curiosity. A few years later, I joined the grape boycott.

I am not sure whether or not Mrs. O'Neil inspired me to write a protest poem, but I did. I recall seeing two of my teachers surreptitiously sharing the poem and relishing it. I remember just two lines: "The Pope's for peace but not the pill. The birth rate is alarming still." It didn't get me in trouble, but I also didn't get published in the school newspaper.

On my favorite days we read plays. Mrs. O'Neil sat at a desk at the back of the room and appointed a director from our class. Volunteers stood at their seats and took parts in *The Winslow Boy* and *The Glass Menagerie*. Afraid to read in class, I did not get called on, but one day I was absolutely certain I knew the answer to "What is numerology?" I raised my hand. Mrs. O'Neil gave me a wide-eyed excited look with her usual twinkle heralding a momentous occasion about to take place. She carefully moved my body around until I faced the class so everyone would notice me as I supplied the correct answer.

The class put some money together and gave Mrs. O'Neil a Hummel figurine at the end of the year. Was it the one with the kid enjoying a short story or maybe the boy with an umbrella under his arm going somewhere? Someday, I imagined, I would go somewhere.

❋

Every afternoon at Cal Lutheran, I took refuge in the art barn. Like the sculptor Louise Nevelson, I was always cold in school except in the art room. There instructor John Solem gently and passionately opened the doors to my artistic soul.

One day we looked at my paintings outside and he opened an art book, "Look at these artists, Anne," he said. "Emil Nolde and Ernst Kirchner. Do you see how your natural style is similar to German Expressionism?" German Expressionism flourished before the Nazis came to power when their works were confiscated and their lives ruined. Their bright colors and forms expressed the emotional freedom I too was seeking.

Life painting class brought a fabulous array of models, some nude and some in costume. A Persian man with a long hat I expressed in dark cool colors. A large voluptuous woman named Cleo who had been modeling since the Great Depression became cobalt blue, her ample breasts hanging out of her dress surrounded by a bright red background. Cleo walked over to my easel later, admiring my interpretation. John Solem showed my *Spanish Lady* in full regalia to our class. "Look how Anne used the reds and yellows so marvelously, so vivid and alive."

Expressionist Russian painter Wassily Kandinsky fascinated me with his use of color and complexities of forms, especially musical motifs. My roommate Jean and I saw a powerful exhibition of his work at the Los Angeles County Museum. His essay "Concerning the Spiritual in Art" interweaved his artistic and sacred visions. "Painting is an art, and art is not vague production, transitory and isolated, but a power which must be directed to the improvement and refinement of the human soul."

Every afternoon I dragged my body in the hot California sun to the art barn, walking past and envying my classmates lolling around the swimming pool. Once I settled in to paint, I soon came alive. After class, I rushed to the cafeteria before closing time in my paint clothes, exhausted, exhilarated, and famished.

I formed my own perspective in aesthetics class: Art contains four aspects: craft, personal expression, social milieu, and spiritual intentionality. Learning the craft entails perseverance along with finding the right mentors to bring forth one's abilities and nurture one's focus. Personal expression involves claiming one's unique vision. Social milieu is being aware of one's environment and social movements calling for witness. Spiritual intentionality is recognizing and bringing forth the work of the inspired soul at its deepest and purest level.

I was learning to trust the process of dipping brush into paint, touching the white canvas, knowing that a new creation would emerge. However, understanding and claiming my identity, the "me" apart from my paintings, would prove to be a much longer process. One day as I was painting a self-portrait, surrounded by bright reds and greens streaming like an Italian flag, Jerry, my boyishly flamboyant art history professor, yellow hair flapping in the breeze, looked at my canvas as he flew through the room exclaiming: "That's you, Anne! That's you, Anne!"

My Lutheran roommates had Bibles on their desks. One of my new friends declared, "Saints are not in the Bible. They are merely an invention of the Catholic Church." Not having my own Bible, I snuck one off my roommate's desk and began with Genesis. It's a long way from Genesis to Revelation, but I felt now challenged to read it for myself. Later, when I transferred to a Catholic college, I would understand the distinction between what is in the canon of the Bible and what is part of Roman Catholic tradition.

While I sought to understand scripture in a Protestant setting, spiritual writers had already begun to speak to me. Many Saturdays I got lost in the stacks at the Boston Public Library in Copley Square. After making my selections, I'd linger in the Renaissance courtyard, keeping company with Thomas Merton, *Seven Story Mountain*; Simone Weil, *Waiting for God*; Zen Buddhist Alan Watts, *The Wisdom of Insecurity;* and Hindu sage Ramana Maharshi, whose beautiful countenance inspired my devotion. Absorbing the lives and paths of these seekers awakened in me a hunger for my own becoming.

My formal religious training had been limited to catechism classes to prepare for First Communion and Confirmation. What I recall is rote learning from the Baltimore Catechism and colorful film strips about gospel parables. Fortunately, I was an awful rote learner. However, I loved the visuals and presentations given by Father Kane, a handsome young priest whom I admired until the day he disappointed me with the hierarchy of creation. "Dogs do not have souls." How could he say that? Well then, damn the hierarchy!

At Cal Lutheran a new window into faith was about to open in the form of Pastor Gerry Swanson. He welcomed me for conversation in his cozy bungalow known as the Belly of the Whale. Never had I spoken privately to a priest except for confession, yet I felt so comfortable being with this magnetic Lutheran chaplain here in the Belly of the Whale. I remember my excitement as I shared my love of the social witness of monastic Thomas Merton, and Gerry shared the witness of Lutheran martyr Dietrich Bonhoeffer. Hearing and being heard. Integrating religion and politics during this tumultuous time in our country laid the foundation for a bridge between Catholic and Protestant expressions of Christianity, which would affect me for decades to come.

I couldn't get to the Catholic church without a car, so I gravitated to the contemporary services through campus ministry. Change was in the air. I began what would be a lifelong friendship of "faith seeking under-standing" with Peggy and Reg, who were active with Gerry in campus ministry and after college became Lutheran ministers. Campus ministry trips took us to Malibu Beach for candles in the sand and making music together. I watched transfixed as an African-American student moved slowly, lyrically along the beach. Someone called it "tai chi."

One day at our weekly Christian Conversations group meeting, our sweet philosophy professor, Dr. Kuethe, brought in bottles of Jergens lotion and placed them on the floor in the middle of our circle. He spoke about Jesus washing the feet of his disciples and asked us to wash each other's feet. A tall thin male student took my size five foot, fitting it perfectly into his large hand. He smiled with tender recognition. In one passing moment, I felt seen and loved. This simple gesture showed me more about the love of Christ in human form than any sermon I remember from those days. Professor Kuethe, with his soft round face and blue eyes, lit up with love, allowing us to experi-ence ourselves as beautiful and valued.

Though I had many fun times with my four roommates in our dorm suite, I often longed for home. Mulling it over, I decided to apply for a transfer to a school back in Boston for second semester. Then I received a serious note from my godmother, Anna, on blue-flowered stationery, urg-ing me to stay at the California college. I was surprised. She wrote plainly that it was time for me to grow up! I did return to California for spring semester even though I had already been accepted to a college in Boston.

My godparents, Uncle Dom and Aunty Anna, lived close by. Aunts, uncles, and cousins—at one point I counted sixty cousins—filled and nourished my early years. Italian-American families, unlike "nuclear" families, extended their influence in many ways. My mother grew up with seven siblings in Dorchester. After her marriage, she and her new husband lived in her parents' three-family home with two of her married brothers' families. Eventually, to the chagrin of her father, she moved out of the neighborhood to West Roxbury, which was closer to my father's family. As it would turn out, I would need those close connections after my father died. Once my dad was gone, Uncle Dom became the elder of the Ierardi family.

I often visited my godparents at their Victorian house on Anawan Avenue, a perfect name for Auntie Anna's home at the top of the sloping tree-lined avenue. Later I realized the street probably got its name from Chief Anawan, a Wampanoag Chief and advisor to King Phillip, betrayed and killed by the colonial settlers of Plymouth in 1676. As I rushed up the steps to my aunt's front door, passing their huge magnolia tree overflowing with pink blossoms in front of the wooden porch, my aunt peeked through the sheer curtain and hobbled on her bad leg through the double doors into the foyer to greet me with a big hug. In the foyer, a grand staircase led to the second floor landing with a captivating stained-glass window from the art nouveau period.

My aunt, of Irish descent, loved to tell family stories. Her whole face lit up with laughter as she shared a story about her husband's mishaps: "Dom was so upset because he bought a large container of Dragone Ricotta Cheese to make raviolis, and it was spoiled." I can picture my uncle looking like a detective hunting down fraud at the Attorney General's Office where he worked after he retired from the IRS. "Dom told the store manager indignantly, 'I just bought this ricotta and look!' When he opened it, to his horror he had taken the container with the pasta sauce in it, not the ricotta." Uncle Dom gave "Annie," as he affectionately called her, his Jackie Gleason "look," smiling with his eyes, outwitted, yet delighted. I could see he was very much in love with his wife.

As a child, I was in awe of the IRS because Uncle Dom worked there. My early sense of fairness and honesty grew from watching him. He gave me special treasures: an IRS agent's badge, which I kept in a box and sometimes wore, as well as a brown leather billfold where I kept my money. I heard the family warning: "Don't show your tax returns to Uncle Dom. You will pay more!"

No matter what was happening during his workday, he cheerfully greeted me when he came into his kitchen, inviting me to sip my favorite drink: vermouth on the rocks with a maraschino cherry. Uncle Dom would return from the pantry off the kitchen, walking carefully, a bit stooped, bearing the glass of Vermouth and offering it to me as if it were a jewel.

My grandmother MaMa, Dom's mother, taught my mother and Aunty Anna how to cook Italian when she moved in with them in her later years. Aunty Anna became a wonderful Italian cook, and she possessed the patience and good humor to fit in with the Ierardi family. One day, MaMa sent her to the Italian market to buy an eggplant. Two women in black dress were conversing in front of the store. Eyeing this attractive blond, blue-eyed woman leaving the market with an eggplant in hand, they said to each other in Italian: *"Irlandese. Lei non sa come cucinarlo."* ("Irish. She won't know how to cook it.") Anna astonished them by sweetly answering back in Italian and sharing the recipe she was preparing for dinner.

✳

Sometimes you need a substitute godfather when you are 3,000 miles away from your real one. After class one day when I walked into my dorm, my roommate muttered, "You got a call from your godfather."

"Uncle Dom called?" I replied, bewildered. "He's too frugal to be calling long distance." I dialed the number my roommate gave me. It wasn't Uncle Dom. It was the actor Michael O'Shea, playing a trick on me. Johnny had brought me one day to meet him and his wife, vintage actress Virginia Mayo. Miss Mayo was away doing a play in Texas, so Michael called to ask if I would like to go out to dinner with him. He arrived in a black Rolls Royce and brought me to a country club in a ritzy area of Thousand Oaks that I hadn't known existed. Michael entertained me in a quiet way, speaking with a brogue. He told me how much he was enjoying being a part-time detective for the Thousand Oaks police force. He seemed to have an interest in life quite apart from his own ego or accomplishments. I sensed in him a fellow seeker and kindred spirit.

That evening, riding in a Rolls Royce with Michael O'Shea transported me not to just another side of Thousand Oaks but to another side of the universe. The night was dark yet bright as we glided through the hills in his Rolls. Michael told me about epiphanies he had driving through the area, which led him to feel poetry in himself. He was arrested by beauty. I became his receptive confidant that evening.

When we arrived back at the college, I was surprised he wanted to stay with me. He accompanied me to our intimate rustic campus coffeehouse. On the way, a blind student walked in front of us. We slowed down. Michael spoke such compassionate words of admiration for this girl and gratefulness for the eyes we have to see, if only we see deeply. What a beautiful evening it was dreaming with my surrogate Irish godfather!

THREE

Beautiful Mind

We have the mind of Christ.

—1 Corinthians 2:16

An artist should paint as if in the presence of God.

—Michelangelo

My sophomore year at Emmanuel College in Boston could not have been more different than my year at Cal Lutheran. Just getting to school turned into a hardship, especially in winter rain and snow. I took a bus and a trolley—my left arm barely grasping my black art portfolio and my right arm carrying books and a purse—then walked the last mile onto the campus. Entering the wrought-iron gates brought me face to face with a life-sized statue of Christ with outstretched arms. I had transferred to the Catholic world of Emmanuel College and the Sisters of Notre Dame de Namur. An ancient elevator brought me to the art department on the attic floor of the administrative building, a massive Gothic structure in the Fenway.

I never would have gone to a Catholic college if I hadn't gone to a Lutheran college. In retrospect, California jump-started me on the road to my quest for meaning. Art, religion, and literature wrestled within me as I sought answers to big questions about such things as suffering. I was discovering people living a faith that not only mattered but made a difference. There was no question I would choose another small liberal arts Christian college—this time in my own backyard—to further develop my faith, not in the parochial Catholic Church, but in the Church of Vatican II, of Merton and the Berrigans.

Sister Rose was tall, thin, and poised. She moved as if holding her body inward in the simplest and humblest of ways. Her hair was gray, she wore a simple dress, and held a small black purse in her hands. The cross hanging from her neck bore the motto of the Sisters of Notre Dame: *"Ah! qu'il est bon le bon Dieu!"* (Ah, how good is God!) She was not young, though she could giggle like a teenager. She had earned three doctorates—in science, philosophy, and theology—yet remained so unassuming. She taught the required class Anthropomorphic Dimensions of Man. I was amazed at the scope of learning in that one course; eleven required books included works on existentialism, mythology, world religions, theories of belief and unbelief, biblical perspectives, and historical and scientific perspectives. We read Albert Camus, Teilhard de Chardin, Mircea Eliade, Bernard Lonergan, and Gabriel Moran. Sister Rose unlocked and expanded the treasures of Catholic intellectual thought, placing them in the context of world religions and philosophy.

In our first class, Sister Rose drew a circle on the blackboard enclosing the words faith and reason, both equally important in coming to understand life's meaning. She had based her doctoral dissertation on six words from St. Paul's letter to the Corinthians: "We have the mind of Christ" (1 Corinthians 2:16 RSV). How awesome! Faith is to be cultivated with our minds as well as our hearts. Her dissertation concluded with these words: "Christian life is basically maturing in Christ to the 'stature' of Christ, for it is a call to such maturity: a maturity tested by one's manner of judging and loving, a maturity by which one comes finally to have 'the mind of Christ.'"

Sister Rose preached through her mind and heart that we too have the mind of Christ. The revelation of Christ is ongoing; it's a living thing. Where it calls me is a mystery. What matters is my commitment to follow the call. Like Mary, I pondered all these things in my heart.

My mind that first semester felt as scrambled and diffused as a kaleidoscope with all the little colorful pieces collected at the bottom. Now my intellectual capacities rose bit-by-bit, turning into a beautiful mosaic, metamorphosing into intentionality. My mind stretched like an elastic band to embrace knowledge as catholic and universal, opening wide to our potential not merely as individuals but as part of the communion of minds and spirits of all humanity, past and future. I imbibed freedom of the mind as a beautiful thing and once it grew inside me, I held it for life.

Sister Vincent de Paul, chair of the art department, had white hair that stuck out of her black veil in an unruly fashion; she was an authentic blend of artist and religious prophet. Some of the art majors, especially those who had attended parochial schools, poked fun at her for being a bit scattered and old-fashioned like a Miss Marple or Sister Wendy. I thought the world of her. She embodied a way of life I could imagine for myself, not in the particularities, but in the essence. A vocation. Sister Vincent believed in the duty of the artist to teach and change the world. In design class, she showed us the Ben Shahn portrait of Sacco and Vanzetti: "The day these prophets were condemned, Shahn was there on the Boston Common to record this moment in history. As artists, don't worry about eating lunch. You need to put art first." I confess, though, I never did skip lunch.

In her class on teaching art to young people, she told us that the most important thing is to find something good, something special in each art piece, thereby encouraging the child. One can find the bud of art in even a scribble. And she was right. I learned to perceive and uncover that thread of potential in each person I would come to teach in the future.

Sister Vincent designed the chapel at the convent where she lived in Ipswich on the North Shore. After teaching all day, she traveled an hour back home to spend evenings painting the Stations of the Cross in the fine detailed medium of egg tempera. One day she brought us to this amazing chapel. The magnificent stained glass, imported from Italian artisans, created an awe-inspiring numinous experience. My later foray into icon and fresco painting had its roots in Sr. Vincent's love of many forms of Byzantine and Renaissance art. These women modeled what is possible when faith and artistic expression are intricately linked, impacting my future as an artist with spiritual yearnings.

Even though back in Boston, I still felt lonely. I missed the friends I had made in California, the art studio, and the freedom from not living under my mother's roof, along with the extra time that living on campus afforded me there. While I knew Emmanuel College was a good direction academically, I just had to get out. Late fall and the weeks approaching the holidays were a bleak and bluesy time spent hanging out in my room with Billie Holiday. Perhaps it was the memory of my first Christmas without my father. Anthony had documented those days long ago in slides I would try to forget: me in an ugly Brownie uniform, holding a doll, and looking thin, forlorn, and forgotten.

The typical Protestant cross is barren. Why? Why not? Didn't Christ rise from the dead? The tortured body of the crucifixion was viewed as bad theology to the Protestant reformers. They wanted to rid themselves of the excesses of ornate churches, the suffering Jesus, and statues of all those crazy saints and mystics that I loved but that mystified my freshmen buddies at Cal Lutheran. Roman Catholics before Vatican II embraced suffering as redemptive, only possible through an experience of love. Catholic traditions, such as walking the Stations of the Cross and devotion to the Sacred Heart of Jesus, originated centuries ago when people lived visual, aural, and communal lives. As an artist, I desired to integrate a more "catholic" vision into my soul and psyche. I needed the freedom of the individual conscience to think for myself and discard what no longer fit me. I needed the beautiful mind I found at Emmanuel, but I also needed the beautiful human connections I had formed at California Lutheran.

I met with the academic dean and the president of Emmanuel to request a junior year leave. I had never been in the president's office, so I felt a combination of nervousness and awe. The furnishings were formal, but in a feminine way with large patterned upholstered chairs. The two sisters invited me to sit down and tell them my wishes. While many students did a year abroad their junior year, no one had ever returned to a school they had already left. Certainly, no one went to a Lutheran school from a Catholic college! However, the Sisters of Notre Dame de Namur were women committed to social justice and ecumenism. I left with their blessings and returned to Thousand Oaks.

FOUR

Hollywood, Lovers, and other Strangers

"AH-NNE," HE EXCLAIMED IN HIS THICK DUTCH ACCENT, WHICH OFTEN sounded like he was on the verge of an attack, "What did 'de goode nuns' teach you at Emmanuel? A pot should be elegant. Is that what de goode nuns in Boston teach you: Art accidental?!"

Back at Cal Lutheran, I still frustrated my sculpture and pottery professor by persisting in doing things my way. I couldn't help it! Sir Bernardus Weber was an old master from the Netherlands. He taught his classes in the European tradition, disdaining modern ways and dismissing female art students. I struggled mightily with my southpaw hands to center the clay, but the heavy round cement wheel that I had to spin with my foot always seemed to ruin my momentum. Painting involved seeing, feeling, and the courage to experiment. Pottery and sculpture required earthier, technical skills. Some days, the best I could do was to stay out of his way.

After throwing the clay, the next project was creating a plaster sculpture in relief. My complex design necessitated a lot more than one layer of plaster. Mr. Weber, his face becoming redder by the minute, swearing under his breath in Dutch, couldn't get the damn thing out of the sandbox. He took a garden hose to my sculpture, which came out in at least two pieces, the larger piece being too heavy for me to even lift. I didn't know whether to laugh or cry.

Quite "accidental," I did learn something from Mr. Weber—not from the studio, but from his classroom where he showed us black-and-white Dutch films made during and after World War II and the Holocaust. His voice grew soft, his eyes filling with tears as we saw the statue at the railway tracks commemorating the children who had been transported to the death camps.

One day Mr. Weber called me into his office. I anticipated some kind of artistic advice or maybe a change of heart about my work. But no. "Ahne," he said in a kind almost sweet voice. "I know I saw you with that boy the other night on campus." (Mr. Weber's house was across the street from the campus, so he apparently saw me with a tough but sweet little guy from Gary, Indiana, who slept in his car near the campus.) "But I think you are going to be a nun." Somewhat stunned, I said, "What makes you think that, Mr. Weber?" Then he replied with a twinkle in his eye: "I just have a feeling."

The dialogue ended there, but what "freaked" me out was that I was indeed experiencing changes in myself of a spiritual nature. Amazing that Mr. Weber saw and cared enough to speak to me even though I couldn't grasp what this strange "calling" was all about. In spite of my fear of him and his gruff manner, I also saw in him a quality of kindness and genuine affection toward me.

I had just devoured Nikos Kazantakis's book on Saint Francis, opening my heart to joy and the feeling of desiring to give of myself to God. Soon after, Pastor Gerry invited all of us involved in campus ministry to visit a Catholic monastery nearby. It was early evening but still light when we approached the picturesque monastery on a hill amidst palm trees and white stucco buildings. The brothers came out in their black cassocks and warmly welcomed us. We joined them at Mass followed by refreshments. They put on hilarious comedy skits and ushered us on a tour of the grounds. By then it was growing dark, yet I saw light, an illumination that filled me with longing, a deep connection to the presence of God. I did not want to leave. I felt I belonged.

During college breaks I often stayed at Johnny's apartment in Hollywood. He took pleasure in showing off his sister to his wide circle of friends. He seemed to love everyone. Johnny had a soft spot for stray people like the blond beauty he rescued from Redondo Beach whose mother had committed suicide. He brought him to campus and took us both to dinner. I had little in common with a surfer boy and felt puzzled and awkward with him being with us.

When Johnny first arrived in Los Angeles in the late sixties, my mother went out to visit him in the Hollywood Hills where he rented a gorgeous house. She found one of Johnny's stray young men hanging out at the house. He had overstayed his welcome, and other guests would be arriving the next day. My mother simply announced to this fellow that it was time to pack his bags. To my brother's relief, he was gone in less than a day.

Actress Janice Carroll always had a bright smile for me. She dressed in jeans and drove a truck, selling antiques. One day Janice took my hand and began reading my palm. "You will never have an alcohol problem because your stomach will have an early negative reaction." Unlike the other women, she did not put on any feminine airs or wear artsy jewelry. Later I would figure out what was going on with Janice.

Johnny invited male couples and straight couples to his apartment, though I had not yet become aware of sexual identity. My brother never spoke of it nor explained his relationships to me. Johnny's parties with people from "the industry" fascinated me with stories about the stars of the golden age of musicals and what they were really like. He took me to studios— Paramount, Universal, and MGM—sometimes right on the set while they were filming the *Lucy Show*, the *Carol Burnett Show*, and *Golden Girls*. In the evenings, Johnny's passes got us into the movies nominated for the Oscars.

One spring break, I took care of a dachshund named Valentine, house-sitting for a couple in the industry. I relished perusing their wonderful collection of signed first edition books and swimming in their oval-shaped pool. The day I left, Valentine jumped into the car with me. It was a sad goodbye for both of us.

The first day of junior year registration, Jerry, my playful art history professor introduced me to a hippie-looking fellow with long dark hair and a thick full beard. "Hey, Wolf, meet Anne." Wolf smiled with a bemused glance at Jerry and shook my hand. We became friends. An intense guy who spoke of his interest in politics, psychology, art, and theater, he told me his childhood mirrored reruns of old fifties television shows. In analyzing his mother, he concluded that she lived through him. Wolf introduced me to the psychologist Wilhelm Reich and his theories about body armoring. What interesting ideas, I thought. He played the Cheshire Cat in *Alice in Wonderland* and appeared in my dorm in costume carrying his tiger tail. He left at midterm to go to the Art Institute in San Francisco to study film. "The new medium," he declared.

Missing Wolf, I discovered Bita, a dark complexioned, intense, shy woman from Iran. The Shah of Iran was then in power. Bita went to a protest in San Francisco and put a bag over her head, fearing that her family back home would be targeted for reprisal. She seemed so lost. I suspect she would have been lost anywhere in the world. Time with Bita passed without notice, the hills blossoming with yucca trees and road runners scurrying through the dry land. Gophers popped up to look at our happy wanderings.

I tried to understand Bita's background without prying, and I shared some personal artistic photos with her taken by a guy in my art class who did photography. He was the son of the lady who ran the store where I bought my art supplies, and in the words of my roommate: she was a "good Christian woman." Yet while she was being a good Christian woman, her son was enjoying himself at home. I agreed to pose for him. I thought I had an attractive body, and he assured me the photos would be aesthetically shot, showing form and not identifying personal features. I have no memory of the actual shooting, but I do remember quickly taking off my clothes in front of him and his girlfriend as they lay in bed one afternoon. I said something awkward like, "Is this what you had in mind?" "Yes, that's fine," he said, looking embarrassed.

He later showed me a proof of the photos. I was proud to have done this for myself, not for him. I did feel a bit uncomfortable seeing his mother afterward when I went to buy tubes of paint.

I only showed the photos to Bita. She liked the shots but was rather taken aback when I revealed to her it was me. Muslim culture has strong taboos about the female body. One day I asked her to go swimming with me at the pool; she was hesitant, uncomfortable exposing her body in public. In the cafeteria she took salt from the table and flung it behind her onto the floor. She explained that salt is precious in her country. This act of defiance, she said, symbolizes the waste and desecration of life she found here in America.

Another time I asked her to read a passage from the Bible for a service I was involved in. In her culture, God could not be accessed through words for God. At the time, I had no understanding of Islamic religion. I felt our friendship was too personal and holy to intrude upon by asking her for explanations. It was a huge step for her but Bita did read at the service. What

I felt about her I expressed in an intense portrait I painted that she took with her on the day we said goodbye and I left California. She left me with a poem written in Farsi. Someone later translated it for me: "that someday we might live together in a little house near the yucca plants in the hills."

At the end of spring semester, Wolf reappeared, walking down the wide steps into the cafeteria. "Hey, man," a black dude said, shaking his hand. "Look at you, you went straight." There stood a very handsome Wolf, clean shaven with a short haircut. Even though I thought I preferred his hippy image, his transformation impressed me. He told us tales about the Art Institute. Nonetheless, it pained me when he confidently declared, "Painting is dead."

Johnny invited Wolf to come with me to his apartment. His roommate at the time was a man from Georgia named Jim. I liked Jim; he was easily my favorite of all Johnny's boyfriends. Jim loved to cook and he could carry on a meaningful conversation. He made scrumptious cornbread in a frying pan. Love was in the air that night for us. When Wolf and I returned from Santa Monica, he attempted to tell me my brother was gay. "Didn't you notice that Jim was dressed in a flowered Oriental robe and he ran and changed it the minute I walked in the door? At the beach and at the apartment, didn't you see the signs?" Wolf was telling me something I was not ready to hear. Why would my brother hide the truth about himself from me? What did this mean? Was he sure? In a way, Johnny didn't hide the truth. He just couldn't say the words to his sister or to anyone in our family ever.

That evening there was a full moon. West Hollywood never seemed so enchanting. Wolf and I talked and walked and walked. We kissed and caressed each other on the lawn of someone's front yard. Later, we returned to spend the night on the sofa bed in my brother's living room. I decided that was as far as I intended to go with a man. I knew my destiny was not to be a wife in southern California or anywhere else. We said goodbye. A few years later Wolf married a nice Lutheran girl. I think her name was Anne too.

FIVE

Energy vs. Repression

SENIOR YEAR ARRIVED—A DARK NIGHT OF THE BODY/SOUL. IN RETROSPECT, electing Contemporary Russian Literature when I returned to Emmanuel was apropos. The course was taught by a little Russian man with thick gray hair and a mustache. At the end of the term, he invited us to his home and served his delicious homemade cherry brandy.

I chose to study the poet Anna Akhmatova. Akhmatova would not abandon love for her people in spite of the Soviets forbidding her to publish because she did not conform to Soviet Realism, another word for propaganda. When they imprisoned her son Lev, she wrote through her darkness in *Requiem*:

> In the awful years of Yezhovian horror, I spent seventeen months standing in line in front of various prisons in Leningrad. One day someone "recognized" me. Then a woman with blue lips, who was standing behind me, and who, of course, had never heard my name, came out of the stupor which typified all of us, and whispered into my ear (everyone there spoke only in whispers):

"Can you describe this?"

I replied, "I can."

> Then something like a fleeting smile passed over what once had been her face.
> No, it wasn't under a foreign heaven,
> It wasn't under the wing of a foreign power.
> I was there among my countrymen,
> I was where my people, unfortunately, were.

Increasingly, the disparity and struggle between the ideal and the real, philosophy/religion, politics/action grew into nagging questions in my mind. While my advisors expected a cumulative body of work leading to graduation, I was just beginning to see and feel myself.

Something forbidden and hidden was fomenting inside me. I wondered about my sexuality. In California I had loved a man, and I had loved a woman. Yet I loved a woman in a way I did not love a man. These feelings erupted in a class taught by a professor who was passionate about social justice and inspired us to care about the lives of ordinary people around the globe negatively impacted by unjust political and social systems, often instigated by our own government.

While moved by this professor's values, I also felt overwhelming feelings of sexual attraction, her body so vibrant and free, unlike my other teachers dressed in more formal or religious garb. I could hardly breathe or focus on her words. I wanted to flee not being able to control my feelings or my body.

A new kind of "call" for embodiment was taking root in me: a coming-out siren that could not be suppressed. In spite of the trappings of the ecclesial past surrounding me, the essence of my humanness broke through, taking root in my body, a woman's body. The patriarchal

Church intones, "Take this and eat. This is my body given for you." Was I not invited to the feast? Is that why communion was offered in a tasteless wafer? Surely, that's not what Jesus offered at the Last Supper.

Overcome with hidden emotions and the pain of how and where to open up, I poured my struggles into my painting thesis, "Energy vs. Repression." The faculty didn't seem to understand or value my project. I felt betrayed by Sister Vincent, my project advisor. She said very gently that I wasn't known by the other faculty; my art work was always done at home since I was a commuter. She told me to go meet the other faculty. I never did. I could see with my own eyes how different my work looked from the other students' projects hanging in the corridors of the art department. Their paintings mimicked the palette of their teachers: earth colors carefully drawn in the classical tradition. Fine for them but I heard another voice in my soul and longed to be appreciated for my own creations.

While I felt disappointed by Sister Vincent, I openly fought with the young nun who directed our senior workshop, Sister Caterina. She felt my paintings were too experimental and not focused enough. Unexpectedly, she thought my drawings quite advanced. Influenced by the work I saw in Los Angeles of Kandinsky, I produced several pieces with geometric flowing forms, graphically done with marker and black ink. Nevertheless, I felt attacked and found myself in a rousing fight with this sister. One of my commuter friends, an Ursuline sister with a gentle soul and a wonderful sense of humor, had witnessed the blow-up in class. Her smile mixed with astonishment, delight, and empathy provided me some balm as we sat together talking in the commuter lounge.

I was ready to enact my energy vs. repression thesis! The day Sister Vincent told me my thesis received a low pass, I rushed out of the art studio, took the ancient elevator down to the first floor, and flew out to the Fenway, walking fast before finally landing in the Isabella Stewart Gardner Museum. Like a scene in an Italian movie, my blood was boiling. I needed to unleash this wild woman in me. I had always found strength and peace at this magnificent Venetian Renaissance villa. Mrs. Jack, in her biography, wrote how she had defied Boston society during the turn of the twentieth century. One escapade the press reported "almost caused a panic" in 1912 when she attended a concert at staid Boston Symphony Hall wearing a white headband, adorned with the words, "Oh, you Red Sox."

Just before I graduated, I spotted a poster on the wall advertising the opportunity to spend three months in Italy studying art and traveling. Some school in northern Colorado was hosting it; an Italian professor was leading the program. That would be my graduation present to myself. No more fitting into a box. Expression not repression. *Arrivederci!*

SIX

Italy

Italy is a dream that keeps returning for the rest of your life.

—Anna Akhmatova

You may have the universe if I may have Italy.

—Giuseppe Verdi, *Attila*

Consider your origin; ye were not formed to live like brutes, but to follow virtue and knowledge.

—Dante Alighieri, *Canto XXVI*

WHEN MY PARENTS AND I ARRIVED AT KENNEDY AIRPORT IN NEW YORK, we saw a bunch of tired, bored college students stretched out over the carpet and chairs in the terminal. They were to be among the eighty students I would live with in Tuscany. My mother's worries about the dangers of the pinching and prowling behavior of Italian men had been lifted after the research doctors she worked with at Harvard Medical School reassured her, extolling the wonders of this great opportunity. My mother took pride in her daughter while updating "the boys" in the lab at Harvard over the next three months of my adventures.

After spending a night in quaint Luxembourg, we boarded a train to take us to Florence via snow-capped Switzerland. Our group was exhausted as we scrambled to catch the local train to Figline, already behind schedule. The Italians held up the train for us. Suitcases were quickly passed through the compartment windows. Everyone at the terminal watched with great interest—some cheered, some looked bewildered—as all of us *Americani* ran to board the train.

Paolo, our *professore*, met us at the station. Our bus climbed the steep hill, beeping its horn as it circled each bend, to bring us to the *piccolo villagio*, Figline Valdarno, and the monastery of La Poggerina. A warm welcome to the ancient monastery greeted us in the refectory. The cook prepared a sweet roll with a delicious golden-sweet wine, the first taste of La Poggerina.

From my journal: "I naturally feel a degree of strangeness being here in Italy, yet I feel a strong desire and harmony with these surroundings. People take so much pleasure in being together. They are bound to each other through their emotions, through compassion. I sense a maternal identification with the women reminiscent of my relatives. The countryside is peaceful and still. In the afternoon the people eat, rest, talk, and play. It's easy to lose track of time here. Time becomes irrelevant. It passes quickly here because no one is in a rush."

Half of the week I took courses and the other half I traveled with a few older students: a teacher named Joy and a *paesan* named Francesca, whose grandparents were from the same province of Abruzzi as my maternal grandparents, and she knew a smattering of Italian dialect. Many evenings I walked down the hill to the bar to order a glass of Vermouth, a Perugina white chocolate bar, and to practice my Italian with the locals. The aged lady who served at the bar always gave me a beautiful and gracious smile. I became friends with a man in the town named Remmo. He was serious and kind, dark-complexioned with short hair, rather handsome and thin like most Italians I saw in Italy. We spoke Italian and played ping-pong. I eventually realized he desired more than that from me though fortunately not until the program was almost over. I told him in Italiano: *impossibile.* A wonderful word common in our languages. The day I left Italy he lovingly inscribed a copy of *La Divinia Commedia,* telling me, "when you can read this you will have mastered Italian." He placed a leaf inside the book that still remains.

On Tuesday mornings the piped-in monastery bells woke us at 7 a.m. to board our bus for class in Florence. I rose in Italy without hesitation and even went to bed earlier than at home. My instincts, senses, and body awakened in a totally new way. Eating fresher, simpler meals, drinking only water, local wine, and a morning cappuccino helped my constitution.

Paolo Barruchieri, our art history professor, lectured on Renaissance Art and Medieval Tuscan Art in a classical Renaissance building in the Piazza Republica. Paolo, like many Tuscans, was fit, self-assured, and intellectual. While I didn't easily warm up to him, I learned from him. "The Italians," he exclaimed, "are not romantics like the northern Europeans. They are classical and practical. Look at the Romanesque style. The Gothic didn't flower in Italy as it did in other parts of Europe. The Tuscans are very earthy minimalists." Yes, I concurred, not even salt or sugar in their bread. I would have to wait to get to southern Italy to enjoy some of the sweet treats I was accustomed to back home.

I wandered all over Firenze, in and out of churches, museums, and piazzas. The Cathedral, "Il Duomo," is a marvel with its stunning dome of red tiles and Ghiberti's *Gates of Paradise.* I climbed Giotto's Tower, muttering to myself, "never again," but what a view. I discovered two pieces by the sculptor Verrocchio, my maternal family name. Verrocchio's *David* stood triumphantly in the Palazzo Vecchio, installed at the height of the city's power in 1476. Cast in shiny bronze, the young, small, but mighty David holds the head of the slain Goliath. I came to prefer this David to Michelangelo's famous monumental piece. Verrocchio's David is conjectured to be modeled on his young handsome student, Leonardo Da Vinci.

In Renaissance Art class, Paolo compared three renditions of David: Donatello's and Verrocchio's Davids are at rest, comfortable; while Michelangelo's David is tense, an unsure giant trying to rise above human limitations. Paolo extended his arms in a poised way: "Only spiritual man can be the measure of all things. The problem is in establishing the point between rationality and faith. The solution is perspective."

Perhaps I lived another lifetime in the medieval era, maybe in the Museo de San Marco, a Dominican monastery where each monk's cell is decorated by the frescos of the Dominican priest Fra Angelico. Climbing the stairs of the monastery, I suddenly came face to face with Fra Angelico's *Annunciation*. The holiness of Mary's call transported my soul as the angel Gabriel announced the coming of the Lord. I returned to San Marco as often as I could to enter this realm of holy presence as I realized the miracle had come to me too. I pictured myself copying illustrated manuscripts and sleeping under the image of a Fra Angelico fresco.

Beauty and generosity were present everywhere, in little places and in monumental ones: the old man in Figline Valdarno on a damp day, gesturing at my sandaled feet and saying in Italian that cold makes the whole body sick; the lady peeling my pear at the fruit stand; Teresa Gabboto in Venice bringing me and my friends in from the rain under her umbrella when we arrived at the door of her *pensione*. One day our cook, Pietro, recruited a few of us to pick the grapes on his farm that abutted the monastery. I threw aside my fear of bees to pick bunches of grapes for half a day. Picking grapes, I discovered, is tedious and takes a lot of patience. The cook gestured to me as I was the only one who knew enough Italian to invite the *studenti* to dinner. I replied, *Si, con piacere, Signore.*

Our group was surprised to see the food prepared in a pot hanging in an ancient open fireplace. We sat down with Pietro's family to a meal of pasta with meat sauce, sausage and eggs, salami and pears. I noticed my hosts, like my family, drank their wine with water, but the wine they offered us *studenti* was undiluted. I also noticed their beautiful dark-haired daughter Anna; how well her parents protected her from our naïve American males, who, I was embarrassed to see, were getting more drunk and foolish by the minute.

I took a painting course with an Italian artist, and I asked permission to paint a fresco on a large wall in the monastery. My works done in Italy are all abstract geometric paintings, painting my inner states—the landscape of my imagination—rather than a realistic view of the landscape. I discovered geometric forms as a kind of meditation. Maybe that's why I am attracted to Muslim architecture. (I have always longed to see Istanbul's Blue Mosque and Hagia Sophia.) In spite of my fear of falling, I descended up and down a ladder of the monastery to execute a large area on the higher section of the wall. In this way, I left a part of myself in Italy.

On the last day of our formal program, I sat on the wall in Fiesole overlooking the city of Firenze. The sun penetrated me with radiance and clarity. I beheld for the last time the Arno, the Duomo. Two of my friends stayed on in Italy. I was sad to be leaving, envious of their plans.

To my surprise, I uncovered a fuller dimension of myself in this country that my grandparents had chosen to leave for a better life—a life I would later become the benefactor of. I realized my life was not only shaped by my thoughts but by the places that connected me to my heart, that made me come alive. When I came to Italy I was cautious and tentative, but by the time I left, I had grown relaxed and outgoing, more at home than at home.

Ironically, I lost my desire to paint after I returned from Italy. My senses and eye had so matured with the art and color of the Renaissance that I had no desire to paint nor vision of how I might paint again. I couldn't make the connection between my soul and my paint brush, between my solitary life and the life around me. The sensibility in me had matured, but I wasn't ready to integrate these changes into an art form. Later I learned that Renoir had had a similar experience after visiting Italy and seeing the masters' work. He was forty years old and had become famous for his impressionistic works. He was stopped in his tracks, as I had been, after viewing the works of Raphael, Titian, Botticelli, Caravaggio. Renoir, on returning to Paris, said: "I had gone as far as I could with Impressionism. And I realized I could neither paint nor draw."

SEVEN

Sister Wisdom

Unrest of the spirit is a mark of life; one problem after another presents itself and in the solving of them we can find our greatest pleasure.

—Karl Menninger

THE HORIZON OF KANSAS IS ASTONISHINGLY WIDE—ROADS STRETCH FOR miles with fascinating cloud formations. Calling my attention, the landscape engulfs me, larger than life, lonely but promising. The freedom to begin my adult life is alive with optimistic anticipation.

Becoming a VISTA Volunteer in 1975 was a natural outgrowth of my Christian liberal arts education, the social and political life of the 1960s, and my own inward impulse to serve. Volunteers in Service to America (now AmeriCorps) was envisioned by John F. Kennedy in 1963 as a kind of national version of the Peace Corps. Later inaugurated by LBJ, it attracted young idealistic Americans from all over the nation as well as some seasoned professionals wanting to continue to contribute to the social fabric of the country.

During our training in Kansas City, Kansas, I couldn't help but notice a woman over six feet tall dressed in a Kelly green t-shirt, worn jeans, an FDR button stuck on her tan cowboy hat that she claimed signified French Huguenot ancestry. A polite southern drawl seemed to belie her sense of self-importance and political leanings. Her name was Carrie. She openly expressed her despair at being assigned to a planned parenthood setting in Iowa.

"Obviously, that was a mistake!" she declared. Her Georgia upbringing apparently didn't teach her anything about "borning babies."

"Do you think," she pleaded, "that I could join you all in northeast Kansas?"

Damn, I thought to myself. I hate people who finagle their way into things. Why is she my problem? She can't sweet-talk me. In spite of my misgivings, there was something interesting about this larger-than-life lady that I couldn't ignore.

We all jumped into Emmet's van, a colorful band of regional Americana: George, a tall, lean African-American man from Houston; Carrie, a white southern radical from a small Georgia town; and me, in Carrie's words "a Yankee" from Massachusetts. Emmet, a new VISTA volunteer and retired postmaster, drove us north to our site in his home town.

Passing through Atchison, a town with old brick buildings, I visualized my wild west childhood fantasies, half expecting Wyatt Earp to swagger out while listening for Judy Garland to belt out: "The Atchison, Topeka, and the Santa Fe."

Carrie and George carried on with their colorful bantering adding spice to the stark, understated terrain of winter in Kansas. George loved to provoke Carrie, and her good humor made me less resentful.

"Poor Carrie. You es destined to doom," he'd enunciate with his engaging laugh.

"George, you are so full of shit your eyes are brown," she responded heartily. George became a familiar figure in the all-white small town, living in a hotel constructed of wood at the corner of Main Street.

Carrie razzed him, "I am going to get you a wooden hand to wave to all the people in town."

George responded in exasperation, "Oh Carieee . . . what am I going to do with you, Sister Straight"? His nickname for Carrie. He came up with Sister Wisdom for me.

Northeast Kansas is not flat; there are hills and many different crops. Kansas towns are formed in a checkerboard so I often got lost. Where is east, west, north, or south? I wasn't in Boston anymore.

The early days of VISTA were disappointing. Full of vigor and idealism, prepared to live in poverty and ready to conquer the world, my poor dwelling was not a stable but a former Catholic convent. The white wooden house had rich woodwork throughout the downstairs and five bedrooms with a porch on the second floor. The Roman Catholic Church, with its tall spire, stood next door to us, but I never felt safe enough to attend Mass. In town, the VISTAS—mostly young, educated, and liberal—stood out by our dress and our "foreign" ways. I was accustomed to anonymity in churches. My Catholicism was different too—Boston Irish/Italian not German Midwest. Moreover, my own sexual identity as well as theological questions were simmering below the surface and, unbeknownst to me, finally about to boil over.

Carrie became bored and depressed, holed up in the tiny upstairs corner bedroom, devouring books on Hollywood divas and JFK conspiracy theories while I learned to cook with the help of the *Joy of Cooking*. Another volunteer from Iowa planted a huge vegetable garden, but her term was up before the harvest. So green was I about gardening that I timidly walked over to the rectory to ask Anna, the priest's housekeeper, to point out what was ripe for picking. She smiled with a slight glimmer of amusement and led me to the garden, filling a pot with string beans and loading up my arms with fresh corn. The soil in Kansas was indeed miraculous!

Carrie finally came out of her shell. She cooked my favorite southern fried chicken and introduced me to a new dish: baked pork chops with rice, flavored with Kentucky bourbon. I was shocked the first time I saw her put a cast iron skillet on the lace tablecloth in the dining room. I never saw a roasting pan, never mind a frying pan, placed on our table at home.

"What a hoot!" she laughed, admiring my dry Yankee Italian humor.

Carrie was theatrical, one minute an oversized clown and the next impersonating her favorite actress, Bette Davis. "What a dump!"

She loved being different. Her best friend in Georgia dressed in drag to perform in shows. I appreciated being different from a distance.

Soon I couldn't get enough of her southern ways.

"You can squeeze a penny until Lincoln screams."

"You strain out a gnat but swallow a camel."

Carrie appeared strong but inside was vulnerable and sensitive. Like me, she had lost a parent. Her mother died when she was thirteen; her father remarried and had a drinking problem. She ran away from college to attend VISTA. She seemed to have an inferiority complex about the south, admired the Kennedys, and couldn't wait to visit my home in Massachusetts.

Our bedrooms were across the hallway from each other. One day she entered my room. I was lying in bed. She reached over, her large breasts touching mine. At that moment our breasts merged, drawing us together in a tidal wave of feeling.

Carrie and I entertained ourselves on the front porch. Watching the few cars drive down our street she mocked, "Hey, Elmer, there's those two les-beans on the porch over there." We'd laugh but deep down we wished we were not so alone. Carleen, the town librarian, caught on; she was sophisticated and interested in the topic of sexuality. I was uncomfortable discussing and joking about sex. Carleen, Carrie, and other VISTAS enjoyed the banter and innuendo. A large illustrated book, *The Love That Dared Not Speak Its Name*, came in the mail along with a big box of soaps and bubble bath for us to indulge in. One smelled just like watermelon and another was black with an aroma reminiscent of flamenco.

By June we designed a new VISTA project. The Summer Arts Program included children from ages five to eleven. We painted, made candles in the sand, sang songs, did crafts. Carrie persuaded her new friend, Native American Chief Roe Cloud, to come and teach the children bead work and share his ancestors' folk tales. I taught the kids how to quietly meditate with a candle. One fundamentalist parent questioned me about teaching "candle worship."

Life got better.

"Falling in love again . . . what am I to do? . . . I can't help it." Carrie sang.

In the newspaper, I found a dog free to a good home. She was part Old English Sheepdog. We named her Cleo after the jazz singer Cleo Laine. We raised her and she grew; when Cleo stood on her hind legs, we could look into each other's eyes.

Carleen and Emmett enjoyed the jazz station broadcasts in the evenings from Kansas City and bred in me a deep appreciation for jazz while enjoying their conversation and friendship. The expansive Kansas sky was becoming a haven.

In early autumn, Carrie and I worked at the preschool in the basement of the library. We proved to be a good team; she was more playful and affectionate with the kids and, to my relief, didn't mind taking them to the bathroom. I was creative and planned the activities, played my guitar, and found wonderful picture books with the help of Carleen. Carrie and I painted the walls with a red, blue, and yellow swirling design. I redesigned the preschool utilizing an "open classroom" approach. Now the children could move from water-play areas to dress-up to painting to reading or playing with toys on individual rugs. One of the children from the reservation could not sit still, so she thrived with the new set-up. We picked her up in our government car along with two quieter children. She called me Anne Karate. One day Cleo, a very mischievous dog, ran after our car from the house to the school, her ears flapping and the kids laughing gleefully. When Cleo got loose she headed for the library a mile down the street and sat outside waiting for us.

The last six months of the VISTA project were bright and filled with happy children. One day a week I took classes in early education in Lawrence, including Art Methods for Early Childhood. Now Carrie, Cleo, and I felt like family. At Christmas time we invited the kids to our house for a party. On the way they sang *Do Re Mi* as I carried my guitar.

Unfortunately, our one-year term was up in March, and even through we tried we couldn't get an extension due to local politics. Carrie and I rented a car, packed up our stuff along with her Norfolk Island pine tree, and headed south to Georgia. The children sadly waved goodbye. We were all sad; I was angry too to leave before the school year was over. It wasn't right. We did manage to hire a school teacher to take over, but within a short time, there was no water play, painting, or other areas of our open classroom.

Where would home be now? After several months, we returned to Topeka looking for the magic we shared in VISTA. Yet now our differences betrayed us. We began quarreling. The "real world" was not kind to us. I got a job at Josten Yearbook Company, checking for errors in the yearbooks before they went to press. There was not enough going on in Topeka. We had no friends. We were struggling to survive. Carrie got into her old habits—sleeping too much and smoking pot—which she claimed helped her intellect. I think we both felt conflicted about our sexuality and our futures. For her the conflict seemed to be about her father and men. For me I think the conflict stemmed from my mother and her disapproval. When I brought Carrie home for the first time, my mother said to me privately: "Are you doing something you shouldn't with that woman?"

"No," I said and walked away.

Carrie got an Irish setter that I didn't want, and soon we had a rivalry between "her" dog and "my" dog. Her dog was a fire-red purebred, a needy puppy with health issues, while Cleo was full of mischief, always on the go, barking at cars, and hard to get to come home. One day Carrie dressed up as a stranger with an old gray hat and a trench coat to get her in the house. Cleo didn't recognize her and came in to face a scolding from me.

Carrie graduated that year and we split up. Strange how love and hate walk together in intimate relationships. I found a program at the Menninger Foundation for couples counseling. We each wrote about what we imagined our future would be. She was ambitious in a worldly way and thought about a career in politics, wanted material things, status, even children. My desires were less tangible but no less important: knowledge for its own sake, a life of helping others, art. I pondered in my journal: "I must return to myself. What if I had my personal desires met, would I still need to transcend? Would I still seek God? The answer is yes. Yes, although I'm far from realizing the goal."

We drove back to Georgia. I had to leave Cleo with Carrie's older sister who lived in a suburb of Atlanta. They had a dog as well as space, and my stepfather didn't want Cleo ruining his little yard. I kept in touch once in a great while, but I never returned to Georgia. I felt sad and guilty for abandoning my dog.

The persons we find when we "come out" sexually and emotionally are often not the same people we stay with for the long haul. Needless to say, our society, families, and church didn't help us much in those days. We had to be inventive, sometimes engaging in risky and/or courageous acts. On the outside, Carrie had an "outrageous" personality that loosened me up to take the plunge. But our inner lives carried us to divergent roads in the scheme of things.

EIGHT

The Moon, My Mother, and Me

Aiutati che Dio t'aiuta.
God helps those who help themselves.

MY MOTHER HAD BEEN DYING EVER SINCE I WAS A CHILD. WHY THIS WAS remained a mystery. For many years I carried a deeply hidden anxiety that she could die instantly. I feared she might meet with a terrible tragedy and never return home. Dreams exerted a vivid presence in my psyche. While I have seen photos of the inside of my home as a small child—the brown two-family—I do not hold clear pictures in my mind. I imagine the rooms to be dark. My mother kept on a nightlight in my bedroom.

After I fell asleep, the boogieman chased me down the street and stole me from my family. In one dream, my mother was shining my shoes for Sunday Mass on the white wooden cabinet in the corner of the kitchen. She didn't see the boogieman about to grab me; she didn't hear my cries. Another time, my older brother Johnny was putting on his socks in the bedroom. Likewise, he didn't see the boogieman waiting for me in the hallway; instead he told me to leave him alone.

Perhaps the girls next door told me too many frightening ghost stories. Perhaps I sensed trouble coming from our landlord who lived upstairs. I heard from my family how Mr. O'Reilly harassed my mother when he was drunk, calling her a "wop" as he stumbled upstairs to his apartment. She tried to ignore him. My father did not like to stir up trouble. The rent was cheap because my mother's family had a connection with the landlord's father, "old man O'Reilly."

I grew more dependent on my mother after my father's death, and I imagine she also did on me. From that early age, I cultivated the habit of sparsely sharing whatever I thought might be upsetting to her. Like George Washington, also born under the sign of Pisces, I will not tell a lie but that still leaves much to omit. My mother didn't say everything in words either, though she expressed herself plenty.

After I was away in my mid-twenties, I returned home to find a little card on my bedroom bureau leaning against the Infant de Prague statue. My mother had placed a prayer card to St. Jude there, the saint of lost causes. Nothing was ever said.

In my thirties when I began to see a therapist, I asked my mother about the nightmares on Willow Street. "Yes," she replied in her usual matter-of-fact way, "you were always scared." That was all. I never attempted to get to the why with her—my mother not being a "why" type of person, unlike me who persists in wondering why. In her later years, her response to death or tragedy was "this is our life."

As it turned out Ma made it shy of two months to age 102. We were to course many miles over many decades of joy and pain, sometimes on parallel tracks and sometimes on opposite tracks.

❈

In my teenage years I began to seriously study astrology. In my neighborhood, I found Maria, an Italian-American Taurus who enjoyed Tiparillo cigars like my dad. Through her patient teaching, I learned the craft of casting a chart, a two-hour tedious labor of logarithms and astronomical tables. We did charts of my family, providing me with my first deeper understandings of personality and relationships.

I would go on to find Boston's astrological world and Isabel Hickey. "Issie" became the "soul mother" to many of the younger astrologers searching for self-understanding and a more perfect world. Each week we piled into a large lecture hall for the "Friday Night Fix" of humor, wisdom, and tools of transformation.

Issie's sun sign was Leo. A larger-than-life, warm, engaging, sunny soul, Issie was evocative like the queen archetype of her sign. She made her pronouncements, direct and certain yet with humor: "Now, don't get mad at the people who sail through life. Nothing bad happens. They are in their 'sabbatical lifetime.' After all, it only affects them every seventh go-round. Down here on earth we are learning how to love." Issie formed Star Rovers astrological group for younger people looking for something different. Issie had a strong belief in the spiritual nature of astrology; she was a pioneer in that field. She wrote an inspirational book titled *It Is All Right*, which she inscribed in the front of my copy, "To Anne, May you find some of the answers in this book. Bless you. Isabel Hickey."

Over the course of seven years, I taught my own class at our local adult education program and then at my apartment. My cousin Teresa liked to kid: "All I could hear was laughter in that group you called a class!" Around 9 p.m. my partner Judy would join our class with a tray of coffee, tea, and goodies. "Here comes Missy!" razzed my middle-aged, married women students, delighted at being waited on.

Astrology became a tool for their growth and enjoyment, a break from their ordinary lives. Each woman had a crisis or, as the Chinese sage would say, an opportunity. Rose, a middle-aged housewife, lost her husband suddenly after he had a heart attack coming down their front stairs. With encouragement from the group, she learned how to drive and went to work full time. Catherine had teenaged children and a husband whose drinking was out of control. She got stronger and more able to protect herself. Jan had five needy adult children and decided the time had come to "divorce" her children and pursue her own college degree. Judy and I taught her meditative techniques. When her kids were too demanding, she'd hold her hands up to her ears and say, "The wind blows in, the wind blows out." We celebrated our birthdays together. I cast charts for all their children.

Astrology groups provided a kind of extended family for me, except that I was no longer the youngest kid. I came alive when I talked about the signs, planets, and aspects and how they worked in our lives, how we had choices. We don't have to accept our lives without question because we were born in a certain neighborhood or into a certain family. Each of us has a unique personality and potentials waiting to be freed. As I saw my students grasp a deeper and fuller expression of their lives, I felt a profound sense of gratitude and gladness. Without realizing it, I was living this unique calling, in the words of spiritual writer Frederick Buechner: "The place God calls you to is the place where your deep gladness and the world's greatest hunger meet."

My mother and I share the same moon. Picture a big wheel at an amusement park with 360 degrees of possibilities. You gamble your money and cross your fingers even though your head tells you that your chances are pretty slim. An astrological birth or natal chart contains these same 360 degrees, and while family members often have planets in the same signs, it is significant that my mother, my older brother, Johnny, and I all have the moon within one degree in the sign of Libra.

Not only did my mother and I share the same moon in Libra, signifying sensitivity and intuition regarding each other's feelings, but our moons were aspected by what the ancient astrologers called an "afflicted" moon. Contemporary astrologers call it a "challenging" aspect. I can attest it was both afflicted and challenging! While most people can tell you what their sun sign is, few know their moon sign. Yet often the sign of the moon is more revealing in describing one's personality, especially for women as the moon symbolizes women, mothers, nurturance, and unconscious feelings. Libra is a sign that seeks balance, beauty, and fairness in relationships. Just because Libra desires balance doesn't mean they have it! In real life such balance rarely occurs, especially with a challenging moon and a challenging life.

At times, I feared the strength of my mother, who appeared larger than life, full-bosomed, towering over my thin, bony, child-like torso. I knew how to behave in her presence and "look presentable as other people are looking at you." After all, her sun sign was Capricorn, the sign of managers and leaders, while in contrast, our moon sign in Libra aimed to please others and exist in harmony together. The connections my mother and I carried mostly unconsciously through the early years of my life resulted in our need for each other as well as our difficulties with each other.

Our family's life was pink with promise in 1953 when my mother birthed me. My brother Anthony, ten years older than me, recalls it as the time Lucy Ricardo was pregnant with Ricky Junior on TV. Desi Arnez crooned "There Is a New Baby Coming to My House." Anthony said, "Ma had you in the winter of 1953. I was so excited that day I missed the bus for school. I bought you a tiny golden ring with your initials AMI on it." I still have it.

It's not that my mother didn't have a sense of humor; she had to, given the fact that my father with his Groucho Marx humor, also inherited by my brothers, was quick-witted and loved to tease. She admitted, "I am the battleaxe; your father is the softy." After my father's early death, Johnny teased, "you'll live a long time; only the good die young."

Since my mother had "eyes in back of her head," as in the Woody Allen movie *New York Stories,* I could imagine her voice zooming in on me above the Boston skyscrapers. As a child, my mother and brother dressed me in fancy clothes. Tony, my stepdad, recalls visiting my family in the sixties: "You were so full of starch you could hardly move!"

Me, who loved to move, climb trees, and play ball. I donned an engineer's hat when playing with my brother's electric Lionel trains. I collected Wild West cards and dressed in cowboy clothes complete with hat, holster, and a tan suede vest. I was a baseball star and assigned my cousins Paula and Janice to play Mickey Mantle and Frank Malzone. My cousin still remembers these escapades and how she impressed her boyfriend with her baseball knowledge. Even my mother enjoyed telling people about the day I was anxiously waiting for my father at the curb in front of our house: "My daughter went outside to meet my husband, and she wouldn't tell me where they were going. She came back with a football helmet and red shoulder pads! Of course, my husband liked the idea, always catering to her."

"Anne, it's no use. You ought to know by now not to argue with your mother," Tony intoned. My mother was married fifty years: twenty-five to my father and twenty-five to Tony who married my widowed mother when I was sixteen. Both men complained that she ruled the roost, yet both depended on her. In our finished basement at the bottom of the stairs, a plaque read: The Opinions of the Husband of the Household are not necessarily those of the Management.

My mother had dark brown hair, almost black. She was of medium height with a strong frame. She ran the household, paid the bills, balancing the checkbook to the penny. She cooked never-fail delicious Italian and American dishes: cheese ravioli from scratch rolled on the wooden board as big as our table, sauce by the bucket-full, cavatelli by hand, pizzelle, and ricotta pies.

Her mother, Carmella, died when my mother was in her twenties, many years before I was born. A year before my mother died, she told me, "My mother was laid out on Mother's Day at our house. My mother used to say that God would bless the stones I walked on because I cared about people."

Women were strong in my mother's family. Carmella was the mainstay, growing vegetables that my mother sold door to door and developing the successful family construction business with her husband, four sons, and her oldest daughter, Rose, who ran the office. An independent and shrewd business woman, my mother's sister Aunt Rose drove a large black Cadillac with wings on the back. She wasn't afraid of anything or anybody. She told me when I visited her in Florida after she retired, "I drove the truck every Friday with a loaded gun on the seat to bring the payroll to the men."

I imagine my mother carried deep feelings about her value as a home-maker, common to women of her generation. "Do you remember," she asked me, "when Mrs. Davoli, who you probably were too young to know, came over for a visit. She took her finger and rubbed it on my chandelier and said, 'Look at this dust.' I was so mortified." I wondered to myself how Mrs. Davoli managed to spy on my mother and locate the one spot that she missed. I am certain she did so smug with glee. My brothers joked, "Let's rope off the living room like they do in museums." Even to-day, Anthony carefully pulls down shades to keep the sun off the fabrics. "I inherited the oriental rug gene," he says dryly.

My mother, born under Capricorn, the sign of the goat, often voiced, "he got my goat." Indeed, my brother Johnny loved to get her goat, loved to tease her. When Johnny was in his fifties, he attempted to talk with a counselor friend. He called my mother from Los Angeles and told her what the therapist said: "You ruined my self-esteem." Johnny delighted in sharing her response, "You are so full of shit!"

Her people from the region of Abruzzo are "hard on the outside but soft in the inside." One day when I was living on the Cape and working on an art project, my mother climbed the narrow stairs to my attic studio with difficulty and looked admiringly at the painting on my easel. "How do you do all this? Rome wasn't built in a day." I couldn't believe my ears.

NINE

Consolation

What though the radiance which was once so bright
Be now for ever taken from my sight

—William Wordsworth

WHEN MY WORLD, ALONG WITH THE REST OF THE WORLD, WAS FALLING apart, her house at Thirty-Nine Chickering Road remained my slice of Camelot. Auntie Rosie Angel was my father's youngest sister. At a certain age I was disappointed to learn that Angel wasn't my Aunt's real name. My brother Johnny, whom Rosie called Johnny Boy, had initiated the myth by naming her Angel as she was so fun-loving and special to us kids. Even my mother enjoyed her company, though she commented one day, "She's no angel." But Auntie Rosie Angel was an angel for me as a child.

The low fence in front of their ranch home was covered with pink roses, pansies showed off their purple and yellow faces, and tall pines surrounded the back yard. A slate walkway of blue and pink led to their brick front stairs. As a three-year-old, I was somehow fascinated by their peat moss. "Anne Marie would come over and ask to see the peat moss, so Uncle Con Con and I, Auntie Ro Ro, would bring her over to the side of the house to see the bag of peat moss," Auntie Rosie recalled with affection.

Rosie married Constantine Pappas, a Greek-American, who had been an Air Force man during World War II. They lived near us in the suburb of Dedham, a place my grandmother MaMa called "Dedhama."

While I heard whispers by the relatives that she "couldn't have children," one Christmas I was excited to meet my new cousin. They named him Leslie. He wore a bright red suit like a miniature Santa Claus to gift our family. He was two years old and I was five. I took a shine to him. As sensitive and imaginative children, we became like brother and sister. We would later shorten our names to Les and Anne. I coveted his train set. He played with my Barbie dolls. Auntie Rosie baked Toll House cookies, powdered-sugar Greek butter cookies, and my favorite fried chicken. A whiff of freedom filled my being, as Leslie and I were left alone to play and imagine in their knotty-pine basement. One Halloween we heard banging at our back door; there was my aunt dressed in a khaki uniform with a horror mask wielding a shillelagh.

The summer after my father died, Auntie Rosie Angel asked my mother if I could go with them on their family vacation. On a sunny day, Uncle Connie drove his Pontiac to Pleasantdale Road to pick me up. I jumped in the back seat with Leslie. Uncle Connie drove north to New Hampshire to a resort named Point Breeze on Lake Wentworth run by the Stevens family. Old man Stevens had some missing fingers due to an accident. I was curious and sympathetic as I watched him warmly shake our hands. It didn't take me long to fall in love with Point Breeze. Usually shy and homesick, here I could run around and be me.

Hidden in the woods by the resort, Leslie and I discovered an old abandoned jeep. "All the activities here, and a beautiful lake, and you and Leslie are playing in that rusty jeep," Auntie Rosie laughed. We loved that rusty old jeep, taking turns pretending to drive it. We also swam, won the fishing contest, and went on day trips to Storyland and Santa's Village. In the evening we watched movies and played games in the rec room.

The best thing of all, though, was ringing the dinner bell. We raced as fast as we could to get there before the other children so we could ring the huge brass bell in front of the dining hall. "What would you like today, Anne Marie?" smiled the handsome waiter dressed in a black suit and tie.

The waiters were college students on summer break. "Tomato juice for my appetizer. Roasted chicken with French fries and carrots for my main course. For dessert I will have angel food cake with coffee ice cream."

At home my father would slice the best cut of steak he could find that morning at Quincy Market into tiny pieces for me. He also took the juice of the roast beef and gave it to me in a jigger glass to drink. I loved it as it went down much easier than beef. My brother Johnny didn't appreciate the pampering I got from my parents and enjoyed teasing about it to my mother: "You never used to let me eat whatever I wanted! You are getting soft in your old age. You made me sit there and eat what was on my plate. And you even let her eat in front of the TV when she was younger. She had her own TV table! She won't even taste the vegetables. Just try them. She doesn't like steak or hamburgers. She has warped taste buds. She eats like a Pisces. I have a friend who is a Pisces and he does the same thing with his food. He separates each thing and eats them one at a time!"

Auntie Rosie worried about my distaste for milk. I am lactose intolerant, but no one knew about that in those days. When I was in first grade, I often went and stood at my teacher's desk to ask her if I could throw away the rest of my milk. "Take a sip for Santa Claus and a sip for me," she cajoled. "Now you can pour it down the sink."

One day coming down the steps of the dining hall at Point Breeze, my aunt recognized a woman she knew from Revere. The woman had that witchy look of certain old Italian women—wavy hair with dark wild eyes. They look as if they are about to zap you with the *mal occhio*, the dreaded Italian evil eye. The witch came over and threatened me with what would happen if I didn't drink milk. "They will put needles in you and force feed you."

I couldn't take it anymore. My father's dead and now this? I moved over to my aunt and cried into her large breasts. She comforted me. That was the last I heard about milk.

The following year we returned to Point Breeze—a place of wonder and magic.

[top left] In the kitchen [top right] John P. and I at our favorite Chinese restaurant [bottom] Playing guitar and wooing Judy

Coming Out

The First Call: 1975–82

Identity can be a funny thing. Living in rapidly changing times in my twenties and early thirties challenged me and the groups I joined. I discovered who I was, at that time, primarily by the company I kept and especially by what I held to in my heart. I could be gay in Cambridge and Somerville, Italian-America in Boston neighborhoods, but it took the Italian Lesbians to make me feel OK in both ways, what Italians call *simpatico*.

[top left] Ann B. [top right] Judith at the Italian Festival [bottom left] Me at work [bottom right] Cousin Teresa, my "roomie"

TEN

Half In and Half Out

Love makes your soul crawl out from its hiding place.

—Zora Neale Hurston, *Their Eyes Were Watching God*

HIDDEN IN A CORNER OF ALLSTON-BRIGHTON AT THE END OF A DIRTY factory-lined street dwelled an old boxy cement factory building housing the August Blank Company. I drove my shiny black Dodge Dart, christened Black Pisces by my new girlfriend, to work there in the art department. Shiny black with ivory suede bucket seats and silver chrome detailing, the car was a Special Edition. The front license plate holder showed off my zodiac sign, Pisces, with two black fishes swimming in opposite directions. Tony had bargained with the infamous car dealer, Ernie Boch, to get a good deal for me. Through the plate glass window, I had seen their hands flailing, reminding me of Henry, my boss.

Bored with three previous jobs as a proofreader and desiring a job related to my art major, I girded up my courage to apply for a paste-up position. The company printed on plastic, as in credit cards, calendars, and the Republican National Committee membership card. With confidence, I walked up the steps and declared to the receptionist, "I would like to meet with Mr. Blank." She replied, "Which one? There are seven Mr. Blanks." I soon learned that I needed Henry Blank, one of the two first-generation owners, to beg him for a chance to become a full-time paste-up artist. Henry was a bald-headed man about the age of my stepfather; he referred to us twenty-somethings in the art department as "his girls."

"His girls" were surrounded by men in printing production. Janet ran our art department and shielded us from the daily drama of Henry Blank. We'd watch with anticipation through the plastic window into Janet's office as she and Henry railed against each other about a job contract. Finally, Henry emerged smiling at his girls, sometimes patting me on the head, followed by Janet, turning an embarrassed glance toward us, her sweetness and amiable disposition roughed up a bit but ready for the next round.

One day we "girls" congregated in Janet's office. Karen drew a stick picture on Janet's blackboard of a woman in a boat with a little flag. She named it "Fill-in-da" Blank, the missing daughter of the Blank clan. Under that Diana drew short blank lines for each boss. We nicknamed Henry

"Totally" Blank. The grandfather, who was quite old and rarely appeared at the factory, we named "Absolutely" Blank. Later Janet walked in smiling at her children's antics.

Ann ran the dark room. She figured out early I was in "the community"—her code for being gay. Later she told me it was the heavy brown braided leather wristband on my slender left hand that had tipped her off. Too butch? When I sneaked away to her darkroom to make photographs for my paste-up jobs, I found ways to stay longer. Ann was a shrewd observer of people and their foibles and befriended everyone in the plant. She joined me on my "get out of work" adventures, including African dance at the Institute of Contemporary Dance in Cambridge. She quipped, "By day she works at August Blank, by night she moves to the beat of African drums."

I owe my discovery of dance to Zip. When I had heard in my late teens that an internationally known astrologer and psychologist, Dr. Zipporah Dobyns, was coming to Boston, I jumped at the chance to meet her. I was surprised to find a down-to-earth, plain, "fifties" looking woman with dark pointed glasses and black hair. During the reading, she revealed aspects of my personality I had not yet uncovered.

"There's a fire emphasis in your chart," she told me. "It can show restlessness, a need to try a lot of different things. Enormous versatility. Have you ever tried dancing?"

"No," I replied, somewhat taken aback.

"I don't mean partner dancing. I mean jazz or creative movement. You have a lot of Aries fire in your chart but it's in the 12th Pisces water house. Water can drown out your fire so find how you can release it."

I eagerly took Zip's advice and began creative movement and jazz dance in Cambridge. First, I met Jocelyn, a South African-Anglo woman. Our class tasted partner massage, stretching, screeching like African animals, and leaping like a bunch of gazelles in the great hall of the Old Cambridge Baptist Church in Harvard Square, a place that years later would alter my life.

With the Pointer Sisters I pushed out my chest and stamped my feet, "Yes, We Can Can!" The dances of West Africa shook the fire out in my belly. Our teacher, a beautiful West African woman, was quite pregnant! She laughed at our inability to keep up with her, a moving circle, arms up, feet stamping, hips thrusting as the drummer intensified his rhythms. Not only thinking outside the box but jumping outside the box was another way to come alive, to feel the strength of my joyous body.

A few years later, I attended Zip's eleven-day intensive course at her school in Los Angeles. Held in her inviting and magical home, the space was crammed with floor to ceiling bookcases and a room for a chapel. There were healthy meals coming from the kitchen and plenty of computers for chart casting. We were an international group, including Jacques Brel's granddaughter. Zip lectured on the "astrological alphabet," her unique way of illustrating the psychological principles found in each sign, house, and planet. For example, Pisces is letter 12 because it is the twelfth sign. I have three planets—Mars, Venus, and Jupiter in Aries—in house 12. The 12th house rules what is hidden or unconscious. Zip taught that when a principle is found at least three times in a chart, that trait is dominant in the personality.

※

After returning from Kansas, I explored every connection I could find to be "out" in the gay culture of Boston and Cambridge. I experienced the optimism of the seventies through disco, gay friends, and Jimmy Carter. I needed a time to heal from the loss of Carrie and Cleo. I needed to find like-minded people and become part of the gay community. I moved in with my cousin Teresa in a first-floor apartment of a two-family house, one neighborhood away from my parents' home. Since my mother couldn't understand or approve of my sexuality, and I couldn't talk with her, I needed to find spaces where I could grow into this new identity.

Black Pisces allowed me to discreetly cruise out of my apartment in Roslindale with the radio blasting to meet other gay people. I was amazed at all the places they emerged from. Nancy, my journal writing teacher at the Cambridge Adult Education Center, invited me to monthly writers' potlucks at her home. I discovered Rico and Judith through a bulletin board at a kebab joint in Harvard Square.

One day, working as a dental receptionist, I answered the phone. "Come over Friday and bring a toothbrush. Meet me at Somewhere."

Somewhere was a lesbian bar tucked away in the financial district of Boston. You had to know where it was. While I had been to a couple of bars, this was to be a real date with an experienced lesbian. With "Saturday Night Fever" playing in the background, her expertise and enveloping kisses bewitched me. Wildly passionate, large and warm, she exclaimed: "There's fire in the old girl left."

The other surprise meeting was in Cambridge at a gay social club named Clear Space. Clear Space become one of my haunts, a place where there was no need for hiding. One night they hosted a large exploratory meeting to bring people together. I was thrilled and surprised to meet a man from Roslindale! In those days not many of us different folk were seen out of our neighborhoods. This man didn't own a car and was dressed properly in a Bostonian suit, carrying a black umbrella. He spoke with an intellectual tone, said he worked for the Boston Public Library. His speech was peppered with witticisms. To our mutual surprise, he was my high school friend's older brother, and we had grown up only a mile from each other. Now we both lived a mile apart. I drove John home.

John owned a large brown two-family. I was invited to dine with him. Entering the foyer, I took off my shoes. John was a Chinaphile. In a chest near the door, he stored many sizes of Chinese-style slippers. I was delighted to find a pair of size fives. His house walls were painted red with dark woodwork. All his furniture originated from China. We sat on pillows on the floor and listened to Italian opera—another John passion. He cooked drunken chicken. As the meal began, John ceremoniously brought me a steaming hot towel for my face. The tea basket kept our Jasmine tea hot as we drank cup after cup. Time endlessly flowed just as it had in Italy. One day we were walking in the rain in Boston and John, with his black umbrella shielding us, was carrying on about the opera *Gianni Schicchi*. Half in English, half in Italian he described the story with glee about Italians fighting over the family will.

As much as John was passionate, unique, and funny, he had a dark side, a depressive side. One day after leaving our neighborhood and moving to Cambridge, he held a party. As time went on I found him in his bedroom staring, looking so strange. Had he taken a drug? I sat with him quietly. I felt a dire warning that day that there was trouble brewing under that bright witty exterior. Our shared moments of happiness and spontaneity were never to return. He moved further and further away from his staid Boston life on a path that led him to San Francisco where he could celebrate both Gay Pride and Chinese New Year. Along with two Persian cats, a Chinese tea cabinet, his books and opera scores, he left town. He bequeathed me chopsticks, wall hangings, a large square teak table, a Chinese folktale book, and a cracked porcelain bowl. Another John left my life to move to the west coast.

I tried to stay in touch as I often do with friends, until it became obvious it was futile. When he first moved west, I mailed him the Boston paper *Gay Community News*. At the time I was working at August Blank. One afternoon Janet called me to her office to accept a phone call, a very rare thing. The woman on the other line was the President of Star Rovers, our astrology club. She was married and lived in a suburb west of Boston. Why would Joanne be calling me? She said quickly in her fast pitched Gemini voice: "Who is John Philbrook?"

Stunned, I said he was a friend of mine. She replied, "I have some newspapers you sent to my address with his name on the envelope." I realized that Joanne's last name was alphabetically ahead of John in my address book. I must have hastily written his name down fast and added her address. That ended my newspaper delivery to John, leaving me with a funny but embarrassing story to tell my gay buddies.

At least this episode was more humorous than hurtful. Sometimes discrimination is blatant and sometimes subtle. Later in the eighties AIDS activists would emerge and declare in our faces that "silence equals death." It resonated with me, too, though I was not of that generation or that type of activist. Their anger exposed the many layers of shame and half-truths we had told ourselves and others who only too willingly colluded. In my own persistent way, I committed toward truth-telling and empowering others.

I do miss those gay old days and the special humor my friends and I shared as we navigated the half-in and half-out dilemmas. Who knew and who didn't know? We sometimes misjudged people because of our vulnerability. Each person we came out to provided us a clue about ourselves and human nature. There were the friends and relatives we loved who disappointed us with non-acceptance and others who surprised us and became wonderful allies. A grade school friend and I walked along the shore at Nantasket one day, the beach where my godparents brought me in the summer and taught me how to swim. She shared a story with me about a friend she knew who was gay, giving me the opportunity to open up to her. In spite of her "boy crazy" teenage years, she knew how important it was to be free to be myself.

I remember a conversation I had with an older married man who came out in his fifties. He insisted that our liberation would be costly as we would lose the creative character of difference. I was furious with him at the time. In retrospect, I know what he meant. I also knew the cost of hiding could never be worth the struggle to be free.

ELEVEN

Italian Lesbians

Where I grew up it was a point of honor to declare your ethnicity defiantly. "What're you?" we asked the first time we met another kid. Everybody understood the question.

—Joanna Clapps Herman

ONE DAY FORAGING IN HARVARD SQUARE, I ENTERED A SMALL CROWDED shish kebab eatery. There on the bulletin board was a handwritten note: *Italian-American Lesbian group forming. Call Judith in Somerville for more information.* I called. Judith spoke in a friendly manner, confessing she was only half-Italian and from the Midwest. She gave me an address of a woman named Terry in Cambridge who would be hosting the group's first potluck. I asked my mother to make something "Italian and vegetarian" for a woman's group I planned to attend.

Terry was an Italian-American woman with curly black hair and glasses with black rims. She exuded a wild rollercoaster personality, peppered with humor and a big heart. Immediately, I felt a mutual endearment. Terry was older than the rest of us with her Italianisms in your face. My mother sometimes referred to people like her as "guineas." I guess she thought we should act more discreetly and poised. Terry didn't just "pass" like the rest of us. High-strung, emotional, crazy—all the ways that made her different but alive. She begged me to play my guitar and sing her favorite song by Anne Murray, "You Needed Me." It brought tears to her eyes. It was a rare occasion when I played for someone but I shared my voice with Terry. She became "mother" of the group, helping us to be less serious and more fun-loving. I grew sad when she dropped out of sight after a couple of years.

Judith, the woman I had spoken with on the phone, evidenced the cross between an Italian and a Nordic type. She was strong both inside and outside, blonde-haired, with a large shiny face, passionate and alive, but more about ideas and accomplishments than *la dolce vita*. She was not relaxed. No, she was driven. That is where the rub was for this group: the forces of change meeting *la dolce vita*. In the late seventies, Cambridge-Somerville was the epi-center of feminism, and we, too, would have to reckon with it in our Italian circle.

Moreover, as Italian-American women we also had our challenges. The first challenge was pride and how we fit into American society. Unlike other ethnic or racial identities, most of us were raised to downplay our heritage. Yes, this was a paradox, a mixed message. Don't leave the family and abandon your tradition, but make sure you assimilate and appear like everyone else. When you go to Italy, visit Rome and Florence where real Italian is spoken; don't go visit the *paese*, the poor provinces your family came from.

The second challenge was integrating our identities as lesbians and Italian-Americans. Many years later I discovered literature by Italian-American women that I could relate to, connecting to many of their experiences, including the warnings I knew so well about too much reading. Get a good education, but don't leave the table at home and bury yourself in a book. My stepfather often worried that I would ruin my eyesight reading in bed by flashlight.

✻

In the sixties, my mother was also part of an Italian-American social group. They called themselves "the Suburbanites." The Suburbanites or the "club girls" were mostly relatives and friends of relatives, numbering about sixteen and meeting at each other's homes. The monthly club night occurred once a year at our house. A big deal. My mother embodied Mrs. Clean. Cleanliness was a moral code in our family, topping all Catholic doctrines at catechism class.

On club night at our home, everything sparkled with cleanliness. The chairs were set up in a circle in our living room, with a long table of cannolis, éclairs, bismarcks, Boston cream pie, my mother's signature date-and-nut bread, and her apple pie made with her secret ingredient: brewed coffee.

My second cousin Sue Bello, mother of Teresa who became my room-mate years later, stood out as a "minimalist Sicilian" in our mostly main-land Italian, upwardly mobile, voluptuous crowd. Sue was skinny like me with an independent spirit I admired and adored. Squeezing past the ladies and obediently kissing my aunts, I headed toward the end of the living room to sit next to her. We munched on potato chips together; she confided to me about the girls, poking fun at the ostentatious Italian towers of leaning white and yellow creamed pastry, the constant racket of raised voices, the emotional drama of kissing cousins, in her wry voice.

The Italian Lesbians also loved being together, eating, and sharing stories. Our initial meetings were the liveliest.

Rico, small, strong, and muscular, a Boston school bus driver who worked during the busing crisis transporting children from Roxbury to South Boston, started off: "As a teenager I wore a lot of make-up; my father was a real bastard. He'd say to my mother, 'tell your daughter to take that shit off her face.' I'd be sitting there and he would ignore me. I was fucking angry. I don't know how my mother put up with him. So I got married, a shotgun wedding in the North End . . . only lasted a few months. I couldn't wait to get the hell out of his house."

Rico told a good story, often having us in stitches. She was sensitive, too, and loved music. The first time I ever heard the voice of Dinah Washington was the day I entered Rico's apartment. Dinah's visceral, gutsy voice blended in with the thick dark moxie that Rico projected. Rico enjoyed showing off and laughing at herself.

One day Rico arrived at our potluck dinner with a tall golden bottle of Galliano. "Hope that's OK," she said with a touch of defiance. (I was praying it was too). Judith took the initiative and diplomatically said that we needed to discuss this as many women were dealing with addiction and looking for alcohol-free spaces to gather.

Since each group felt strongly about whether to imbibe or not, we had to break into two separate groups. I went with Rico and the Galliano group, having trouble imagining an Italian gathering without at least a glass of wine. I enjoyed Rico and admired that she was not ashamed to bring the Boston "neighborhood" family dramas into our meetings. I don't remember if we talked about class, but I was aware of the divide between Boston neighborhoods and Cambridge transplants. We were brought up in different worlds. While I was raised in a Boston neighborhood where there weren't many Italians, I had strong connections through frequent visits to relatives. I was thrilled to have Italian women friends and to talk about things that mattered to us: family, coming out, feminism, politics, and of course, food.

One night we gathered at Rico's tiny apartment on Beacon Hill. Barb "the Pisces" was there; she reminded me of an Italian Buddha—happy, dreamy, and content, with a large soft body you just loved to hug. We drank too much wine that night and lumbered down the steep streets of Beacon Hill arm in arm, swaying and laughing like sisters.

After a few years, the Italian Lesbians stopped meeting. The only one I stayed in touch with was Rico, who lived in our neighborhood. Once I reconnected with Judith. She had become an Orthodox Jew, which didn't completely surprise me as we had gone together for a past life reading. A strong memory of a Jewish connection as a Rabbi emerged for her.

Identity can be a funny thing. Living in rapidly changing times in my twenties and early thirties challenged me and the groups I joined. I discovered who I was, at that time, primarily by the company I kept and especially by what I held to in my heart. I could be gay in Cambridge and Somerville, Italian-America in Boston neighborhoods, but it took the Italian Lesbians to make me feel OK in both ways, what Italians call *simpatico*.

TWELVE

The Italian Mouse

Memory is a passion no less powerful and pervasive than Love. What does it mean to remember? It is to Live in more than one world, to prevent the past from fading and to call upon the Future to illuminate it.

—Elie Wiesel

"EDDY," SAID THE MOUSE COYLY AS HE SIDLED UP TO THE FAMOUS TV HOST on Sunday night.

"Ah! Topo Gigio," laughed my aunt Josephine as her large round face turned red and lit up as if she had a personal friendship with the Italian mouse.

Her husband, my great-uncle Jim, whose real name was Vincent, had a brother named Mike, but we called him ZiMichel, which I didn't realize just meant Uncle Mike. Words in dialect strung together had a unique sound that went with the elderly characters who inhabited these names. In "Italian class" in high school, we learned to pronounce every syllable, to open up our mouths to sing each vowel.

ZiMichel was a favorite family member. I didn't see him often. He didn't live communally like the rest of my family, though he evidenced the independent qualities of the Ierardi family, showing up as a sudden urge to not be willing to go along to get along. The stories passed down to me were family legends. There was a great uncle in Italy who played "Yankee Doodle" in church. Did that really happen? Probably.

ZiMichel was a stone mason, creative and devoted to his craft. He lived alone in an old building in Dorchester and carried his tools around in a black satchel. He always had a Hershey bar or two for me and my cousins when we ran into him on school vacations in Dorchester. He didn't keep a schedule or own a car. He just appeared in our neighborhood once in a blue moon like someone out of a fairy tale. He might be friendly for awhile, and then suddenly, he would withdraw into his own world, muttering sounds like "beep, beep, beep." My mother loved to tell the story about the time she spotted Uncle Mike from her window when she lived in her family home in Dorchester. She called out to him, "Uncle Mike!" He gestured by pushing his hands away from her friendly greeting. She closed the window and laughed, saying in Italian dialect *be un gule.* ("Up yours!")

ZiMichel had his own Italian mouse story. Invariably, it came up at our Easter dinners. Aunty Josie, always in and out of her kitchen preparing the feast, loved this tale.

"ZiMichel showed up at our apartment the other day and told me he was trying to find a mouse in his apartment. He became very upset when he couldn't find the mouse. Just as in the *'Pepino Surigile'* song, this mouse was eating cheese and drinking wine and scaring his girlfriend. Finally, ZiMichel gave up and went into the bathroom to shave. Looking in the mirror, he saw the mouse on his shoulder!" Now Aunt Josie is laughing so hard her whole body is shaking, and she is wiping tears with a dishtowel.

Aunt Josie came to this country as a teenager to marry Uncle Jim. Jim was already thirty years old when they married. She raised four sons, kept house, labored long hours at a laundromat; Uncle Jim taught clarinet and made great homemade wine: *rosso e bianco.*

For several years after my father died, we shared Easter dinner at their home. They lived on the third floor of the three-decker. Climbing up three flights of stairs, we would arrive breathless. We always paused on the landing of the second floor, seeing the sepia photographs of relatives of the Lauterellas who lived on the second floor. My brothers found these "old country" photos amusing as they watched for the movement of the lace curtain behind the closed door. Amelia Lauterella was spying to see who was climbing up the stairs to visit Josephina.

As we made it to the third floor, we were greeted with sounds of several clarinets. The boys—my cousins Joe, Dom, Phil, and Anthony —took lessons from their father. Aunt Josie would give us a big hug and whisper slyly, "Amelia will be coming." Sure enough, a few minutes later a small woman with dark wild eyes and white unkempt hair would appear. Aunt Josie feigned a surprised look and, with a twinkle in her eyes for us, she'd say to Amelia, "Go and tell Patsy to come up." Amelia would then barrel down the long hallway toward the back bedrooms and with her large black shoes pound on the wooden floor three times to signal her husband. In no time Pasquale Lauterella would shyly come up the stairs.

Dinner was always a happening, lovingly prepared over several days by my great aunt. My mother would head right to the kitchen, putting on a flowered apron "to pitch in and help"—another of her favorite mottos. A series of courses began with a huge antipasto, my favorite part of the meal. I loved anything salty like sardines, strong cheeses, olives, prosciutto, capricola. Second course was the zuppa, often escarole with little meatballs. I ate the meatballs and left the escarole. Next Aunt Josie brought out a huge platter of pasta followed by bowls of meatballs and braciole (tender beef wrapped with a filling of raisins). We drank Uncle Jim's homemade wine. Fourth course was a roast or two with potatoes, vegetables, and salad. The women cleared the table. The men "retired" to the living room. Soon Uncle Jim dozed off with a cigar in his hands as my brothers and cousins cracked jokes. Later we returned to the table to find a spread of Italian pastries, fruits, nuts, and liqueurs. Often the Lauterellas would join us to play a game of lotto. I stifled a big laugh as Amelia called out her favorite number sixteen: "Sica-Steen Sweet!" My cousins gifted me every year with a huge chocolate Easter bunny. Those days remain sweet in my memory.

THIRTEEN

Laurie's Party

Ah Love! Could you and I with Him conspire
To grasp this sorry Scheme of Things entire,
Would not we shatter it to bits—and then
Re-mould it nearer to the heart's desire!

—Rubáiyát of Omar Khayyám (Edward Fitzgerald)

I met Laurie in a health club on Commonwealth Avenue near Boston University after seeing an ad she placed in the Boston Phoenix for polarity massage. That led to our friendship. Laurie and I exchanged astrological readings for polarity treatments. Laurie was imposing. Indeed, her dark brown curly mane-like hair resembled a lion. She was charismatic, fiery, as well as earthy, with large, strong, nurturing hands perfect for energy-balancing massage. The first time I received a polarity treatment from Laurie my senses became heightened and filled with joy. The next morning, I walked up my street amazed at the vivid brightness of trees and flowers like the colors of a palette of paint. Underneath my densely protected body lay a belly full of joy, laughter, and spirit.

The Sun entered the sign of Leo in 1979 on July 23rd. Laurie threw a party to celebrate the Sun-in-Leo, a cool lesbian party held in a brown two-family house in Brookline with large rooms and a porch. Women seemed to emerge from everywhere; they were drumming and reading poetry. Some I realized had taken their tops off. Were they the Jewish lesbians? They had more chutzpah than my Italian lesbian group. Maybe because they weren't Catholic?

The atmosphere that night was electric. I was nervous but exhilarated. I didn't know anyone besides Laurie and her partner. Fortunately, Laurie, never being at a loss for words, told everyone there I did astrology. A few people came over where I was sitting on the couch to talk with me. Toward the end of the evening a troubled woman with dark tanned skin, long black hair and intense eyes resembling those of a Native American sat down next to me. She launched into a tirade about the terrible day she had been having in Provincetown.

"This morning I was in the A&P parking lot, backing up. The jerks put concrete around the light pole. Wham went my bumper! I fixed them though; I ran over their shopping cart."

To my amazement, she told me she was a medical doctor learning polarity therapy from Laurie.

"I feel like throwing my diploma in the ocean," she said passionately. I listened intently not taking my eyes off her. I had never met anyone like this before, surely not in my neighborhood.

I don't remember how long we talked; the rest of the party had faded out. (My future career in counseling seemed to spring out of such encounters.) I explained to her that astrologically she was in a very important cycle called the Saturn Return, which occurs between ages twenty-eight and thirty-one. She grew fascinated and perhaps a bit relieved. Just as the party was breaking up, an Anglo-looking woman with long blonde hair and full pink lips sidled up to her and stroked her thighs. I got the message she was already taken, though I had no conscious thoughts of falling for her. I didn't fall easily. I was even embarrassed for the girlfriend, though I had no rational basis for that. Time to go. On the way out the door, this mysterious woman handed me her phone number on a little slip of paper. Her name was Diana, and she promised to be in touch.

I left the party in a rather heightened state. A couple weeks later I saw Laurie for a polarity treatment. She peered at me with her curious bright eyes, raising her thick eyebrows and smiling seductively, suggesting something must be brewing between Diana and me. Later I learned she had given my business card to Diana months ago, suggesting she get a reading from me.

About a month later, there I was on a beach in Provincetown, guest of Diana and her lover Melinda. My "official" role was to read their charts. While I didn't find evidence of strong compatibility in their charts, my diplomacy overrode the naked truth: they were not well matched. Plus, I was their houseguest for the weekend.

I also was surprised to learn Diana's real name was Judy. Diana Wild-womyn was the name she took when she moved to Provincetown that year. It was common in those days in radical feminist circles to take new names with non-patriarchal associations. Judy aspired to be "Diana" the huntress. Interesting that her Mars fell in the sign of Sagittarius, symbolic of the Archer, qualities of restlessness, enthusiasm, adventurousness, outspokenness, often acting before thinking. She often referred jokingly to herself as charging on her high horse. Too true, I was to learn.

In early December, Melinda walked out on Judy to be with another woman. Judy became terribly distraught. Many weekends she drove three hours from Provincetown to Roslindale in her beat-up blue Ford with no heat and a bashed-in bumper. She was proud of this car as she had downsized from the fancy Buick her father had bought her. Strange lady.

Judy sought sanctuary in Roslindale with me and my cousin Teresa. After sleeping until noon one day, Judy said to Teresa dreamily, "I could be anywhere." Teresa looked at her and spoke in her usual forthright manner, followed by laughter softening the blow: "Judy, you're in Roslindale!"

One day I drove Judy to Logan Airport in her car as she was on the way to visit her parents in Cleveland. As I drove home, I discovered at the tollbooth that the window on the driver's side would not roll down. A special feature about this car that Judy gloated about was the white spot on the windshield. Melinda, an artist, had painted it to look like bird crap in order to hide the crack in the window to fool the car inspectors and get her sticker. It worked.

In spite of my misgivings about Judy's darkness and confusion about her lost love and identity as a medical doctor, I continued to be drawn to her. I introduced her to my friends and brought her to intimate cafes in Boston. On Friday nights, Judy blessed me with a soul-filled polarity treatment by candlelight with incense wafting, preparing a soft bed on the hardwood floor of my apartment. Her strong hands were gentle and intuitive, guiding my spirit into alignment with my body, dissolving my tension from a hectic week at the plastics factory.

By Valentine's Day our friendship took a radical turn. I was intently focused on preparing pasta for dinner so that it came out the way I liked it: not too "al dente" nor "pasta mooch" as Tony would say in Italian dialect. He also said it to describe a slow-moving person, sometimes in reference to Judy—just the opposite of me.

Judy appeared in my kitchen agitated, almost in tears,

"I am having these feelings for you. If you want me to leave I will."

I grew quiet, needing to take this in while maintaining my cool.

"Let me first drain this pasta, and then we can try it out and see," I replied, or something like that, taking a deep breath. I wanted Judy to stay, but I couldn't just let the pasta sit.

I remember the day as being clear, the kind of day in winter that rewards you when you look out through your old window panes that anything good might be possible. Patches of snow shone on the ground; the air was crisp. We went into the dining room, which was now my bedroom, and made love on my sleeper sofa bed. Our bodies, freed from the repressed loving feelings, knew where to lead us. Spaghetti and wine complemented and completed the experience, just as I knew they would.

After Judy left that weekend, my cousin Teresa watched me in the manner of her analytical Aquarian Sun as I began to carefully navigate the waters of new love with my Moon in Libra poise and need for balance. Moon in Libra thrives on relationships, but it is an air sign, often leading with the head. One astrologer put it this way: "To hear them talk about a potential mate might sound like they're interviewing for a job. They're searching for someone they can glide with through life in glorious tandem while looking as polished and put together as they are."

While my Moon in Libra was the essence of restraint, her Moon in the fire sign of Leo was totally absorbed in the passion of the moment, bringing out my fire and my capacity to be playful.

A couple of weeks flew by. While her muscular body portrayed healthiness and confidence, that was deceiving. Confusion and grief attached to her insides the way barnacles do to mussels. She continued to sleep very late and smoked pot out of her little plastic bag. She followed Laurie to Puerto Vallarta for a polarity retreat, leaving me in Roslindale wondering where this relationship was going—or not going. I felt full and empty at the same time.

"When will you be back?" I asked, trying to be nonchalant.

"I don't know. Maybe six weeks," she replied vaguely.

Before Judy left, a book appeared called *Rolling Thunder*, the story of a Native American medicine man who lived in Nevada. His reservation was about a hundred miles from the US Indian Health Service Hospital.

Judy interpreted this as a portent of where she must go to complete her three years of public health service to compensate the government for providing tuition for medical school.

While in Mexico, Judy fasted on the polarity diet, which consisted of only lime juice, water, and polarity tea. After a few weeks I got a postcard from her of a sunset on the beach. In a few sentences she described a "spiritual" encounter with a French man. I was jealous and confused. I had fallen for her. I wanted her back. How could she be so insensitive!

The next letter I received from Judy contained a plea for goldenseal powder to cure her skin's staph infections. I purchased the costly goldenseal powder, wrapped it in a fine, colorful cloth, put it in a little box, and enclosed a card with words about spending eternity with her.

What had I got myself into? A love affair with someone who was unavailable, in emotional crisis, impulsive?

FOURTEEN

Cappuccino's

SIX WEEKS LATER, JUDY RETURNED FROM MEXICO, ALMOST AS IF NOTHING HAD happened. We resumed our passionate relationship, though we both knew the clock was ticking. She had made the difficult decision to enlist in the US Public Health Service as a lieutenant. Most service sites around the country were in prisons or Native American reservations. Earlier she had considered doing a residency in psychiatry in Worcester and deferring the public health service obligation, but her partner had insisted they move to Provincetown. Judy was also ambivalent as the field of psychiatry was quite homophobic. (It wasn't until several years later that the American Psychological Association removed homosexuality from its psychological disorder list; coincidentally, at a meeting that Judy and I attended in Washington D.C.)

I was amazed to see that Judy had skin sores all over her tanned body. A staph infection. I could not understand how sickness can invade the body in such a quick, visible way. I was accustomed to being protective of my body, afraid to be too physically challenged. Judy had a different relationship with her body. Her medical training added to her understanding of the body as "other." This objectivity frightened me. Once I asked her a question about a problem I was having. The cold way she peered into my wound only added to my anxiety. So different than the soft Judy who gave polarity massages. I didn't really understand this doctor side of Judy, and looking back, I think I feared it and how it might affect our lives together. As time went on, Judy, herself, explored her two sides: Judy and Dr. R.

She saw them as two distinct persons like Judy and Diana. She faced a huge challenge over the years to come to terms with both personas.

Judy (or it might have been Diana) introduced me to psychedelic drugs. I reasoned they might add to my self-knowledge, particularly after my muse, writer Anaïs Nin, whose diaries inspired me to keep a journal, wrote about taking LSD. She believed that an artist can induce such mystical states without a drug. I wondered if I might have that ability. Besides, I thought, I was safe experimenting with a doctor. Wrong.

We visited the New Hampshire mountains for several days in June. One day we tried some LSD. "Diana" had used the drug before and wanted me to enjoy the same kind of mind-expanding experience. My answer came quickly: Anaïs Nin was right. Art and dreams are quite enough for me. My mind was already a kaleidoscope full of pictures, memories, sorrow, joy, wildness, and terror. Judy turned into Louis XIV. My uncle arrived in a black Nazi car to hunt me down. The New Hampshire road I was driving on was a marshmallow as we tried to find a bite to eat. I turned into a child, barely able to ask the man for my favorite flavor of ice cream—coffee.

The night before she left for Nevada, Judy took me to dinner at Cappuccino's restaurant in Coolidge Corner. She ordered a bottle of Chianti to celebrate. Above the table hung a Tiffany lamp that reflected colored lights in the dark *ristorante*. Our waiter approached the table as Judy held up her glass to the light. The waiter said in a concerned voice, "Is there anything wrong with the wine?" Judy replied, "No. I am looking at the face of my lover through the glass."

For me, coming out was a task to be carefully thought out and executed at the right time. Time was important to an astrologer! Judy was a "free" figure-skater moving this way and that . . . maybe the ice was too thin, maybe her gestures were too wild, maybe she would fall on her ass. I might have thought this was a bad time to enter into a romance. Why think? I believed that once I thought things through thoroughly, I was ready to put skates on and perform. Perfectly.

Once again, I drove Judy to Logan Airport. The next day I was back to work at August Blank.

FIFTEEN

The Ultimatum

Living by principles is not living your own life. It is easier to try to be better than you are than to be who you are.

—Marion Woodman, *Addiction to Perfection*

AFTER JUDY LEFT, I FELT BEREFT. I WAS AFRAID TO LOVE SOMEONE AGAIN who seemed to be incapable of loving me. She was absent from my life as often as she was there, and now she had moved all the way across the country for God knows how long.

I consulted with astrologer Nancy Roof who remarked, "Why are you not with Judy? I am surprised you are in commercial art." Looking at my birth chart, she suggested that building a career and status should not be my emphasis. "Your focus is in the sixth house of service to others. Also, with a strong Aries in your twelfth house you are a pioneer called to develop your own creative programs."

We corresponded through letters, but one day she called. She was in the hospital after a car accident. I could tell she was shaken, though she downplayed what happened, offering few details. The next time she called she said, "I want to sweep you off your feet to St. Thomas in November for a week!" How extravagant. Should I accept? After talking it over with Ann at work, I agreed and located an intimate small hotel on a beach in St. Thomas.

Judy's long dark hair was accentuated by her authentic white Mexican blouses with embroidered flowers framing her neckline. When she tanned, she was strikingly beautiful like one of Gauguin's Tahitian women; she belonged in warm climates by the water. I don't remember much about St. Thomas besides colorful boats, sipping Piña Coladas under a tree, and swimming with fishes playing with my toes. The luxury of being together alone was enough. The more we were together the harder it came to be apart. Time for me to act. I would be seeing her again in Los Angeles in February for Zip's intensive training. After that, I agreed to spend a month living with her in Nevada. I quit my job at August Blank. It would be the last time I worked in commercial art, with the exception of freelance jobs that helped finance graduate school.

Before I arrived Judy quickly furnished her government townhouse so I wouldn't think she was totally living as a hippie. While I embraced the "hippie spirit" with beads, bellbottoms, and fringed vests, I liked my comforts at home. She bought a bed, living room furniture, and a set of orange-colored Japanese dishes with peacocks on them. Even so, the apartment was pretty bare. While she was working at the hospital, I spent time across the road drinking tea with a couple of housewives whose husbands worked with Judy. They introduced me to Vietnamese spring rolls and shared the recipe, but the nearest grocery story was over a hundred miles away. It made Kansas look like a metropolis. Judy thought I might be able to get a job at the hospital, like working as an addictions counselor. I had little training or interest in working at a hospital, especially at that time. Hospitals made me anxious, and I hated the smells.

One day we drove sixty miles away to meet the medicine man Rolling Thunder. There the men ate first, then children, then the women. Passing the peace pipe, smelling the sage, and sitting in a circle in a huge teepee was so real it seemed unreal. Later, Judy became disenchanted with Rolling Thunder after he tried to French kiss her.

No, this is not working, I realized after my month was up. I needed to go back to Roslindale and figure out something else. I called Judy and gave her an ultimatum: "Either you leave there within a year or it's over between us."

She knew I wasn't kidding, and she didn't want to lose another partner. Not soon after she found out she could work in a designated physician-shortage area of the country. I set out on that lead, even going to the Harvard Law Library and looking in the Federal Register to find out what would satisfy the government. I found it: Somerville. The town of Somerville, Massachusetts, was one of the most densely populated towns in the state, and because of that density, there was an official shortage of doctors. This is the one thing I am grateful to Ronald Reagan for: his policies took doctors like Judy off the public health payroll if they worked in a physician shortage area. I am not sure where the money trickled down to, but at least I had Judy back, this time for good.

Before she arrived in Roslindale, the USPS delivered many large cardboard boxes to my doorstep. All her worldly possessions. I was glad to see the Japanese dishes survived. Judy moved into my half of the apartment. Eventually, Teresa moved across town. She married a man named Hue whom she had met at a winter camping class in Boston. They wed on a very cold February day in the snow-covered woods of the Fellsway.

[left] Frankie and Margaret at Healthsigns benefit [right top] Barry and Pem at Cape Cod Coalition of Welcoming Congregations [right bottom] Receiving the Welcoming Congregations Award

Healing and the Church

The Second Call: 1982–84

At that time, Catholic women in seminary knew a job would not be forthcoming in ministry. Yet we went to seminary totally engaged in study, in awe of the possibility of Divine Providence, committed to doing our part to create justice in our churches and the world.

[top left] Pavia [top right] Susan cooking at Lenten event at St. David's Episcopal Church [bottom] At Pavia and Lynn's wedding

SIXTEEN

Healthsigns

This puts the healing arts squarely where they belong, for the work of the healing arts is tightly interwoven with religion. To attempt to practice medicine and nursing as if they were pure sciences is impossible. They are also arts and as such are intimately connected with the faith both of the healer and the healed.

—Rev. Granger Westberg

"YOU ARE BOTH TRYING TO BRING BODY AND SPIRIT TOGETHER IN YOUR relationship," Nancy Roof counseled. Judy and I were passionate, curious, and in love. At the same time, our commitments involved a call to the work ahead of us in medicine, counseling, and ministry. In these early days of our relationship, we faced difficulties and setbacks, but we kept on striving, buoyed by each other's support.

We set up Judy's medical office in Somerville, launching our voyage to open a holistic medical and counseling center. We named it Health-signs, signifying health of body, mind, and spirit with astrological counseling (signs). The times were ripe as it was the heyday of the holistic health and expressive arts movements. We designed Creative Wellness for the new methods we were learning, including polarity, body-centered psychotherapy, and humanistic psychology. Each person received a medical evaluation, a holistic inventory, and an astrological chart reading.

We went to Illinois on the trail of a new model of pastoral care, counseling, and medical treatment that Rev. Granger Westberg, a Lutheran pastor, had designed. Though we didn't have the opportunity to meet him, we observed his center and utilized ideas from his training manual to set up our practice as doctor and counselor. Westberg also introduced parish nursing programs, which later spread throughout the country.

One morning Judy's patient told her a heartbreaking story. The woman had worked for the same company for many years only to be told at age fifty-eight that she was being let go. "How are you managing?" Judy asked.

"Doctor, I baby-sit and I sell my furniture."

Judy came home saddened beyond words. Treating the "whole person" is even more than body/mind, but what opens our eyes to see? I introduced Judy to the Paulist Center, a progressive urban Catholic community in downtown Boston. She took a class on the faith of Catholics, which led to exploring the meaning of conversion from her agnostic secular humanism. Her father's father had been a Missouri Synod Lutheran pastor. As a young boy, age seven, her father witnessed his dad's tragic death from tuberculosis. He blamed the church for the shameful neglect and poor conditions that his family endured in the Texas mission field.

Paulist priest Fr. Vinny McKiernan asked Judy if she had told her parents about her upcoming baptism.

"Why no, I haven't," she answered. "Somehow it's been easier for me to tell them I'm a lesbian than I plan to be a Catholic."

The wise pastor said, "That's because becoming Catholic is a choice, whereas being a lesbian is natural to you."

The yearlong catechumenate program culminated at the midnight Easter Vigil service when Judy was baptized, confirmed, and received into the church community. How ironic it was that at the same time I was no longer experiencing abundant life in this church.

I loved the Paulist community, their witness to the social gospel and roots in Vatican II. I experienced joy going to Mass on Sunday evenings, driving into Boston when it was quiet, looking up at the dome of the State House, descending Beacon Hill to the Paulist Center. Increasingly though, I was disturbed with the hierarchical priesthood and its treatment of gay persons.

On one particular June night at Mass, I felt unsettled in a marvelous way. The moon lit up the sky as I walked down the hill. A female chaplain had delivered the homily; I had never seen a woman preach in a Catholic church. From that instant a door opened in my heart and soul.

Like Mary, I, too, was pondering in my heart: Where does a woman's call to ministry begin? Just as for Mary, it often manifests in amazing ways: something unexpected, unconventional, even controversial, and frightening happens; one finds there is no room for the holy presence, the child of light, to enter through the ordinary establishments.

After Mass, I tried explaining my feelings to Judy. "I am that person. God is entrusting me to express the gifts of the Spirit, to claim my birthright."

On Monday I met with chaplain Kathleen at the Boston University Newman Center. I told her how moved I had been at Mass, how I wanted to work toward a master's degree in counseling through a spiritual, holistic approach. She told me about the field of pastoral counseling. Two months later I entered Andover-Newton Theological School, the oldest Protestant seminary in the country, intending to become a pastoral counselor.

Meanwhile, word of our center spread and clients came seeking wholistic ways of healing. One of these was a nun finding herself at a life-change crossroads: to remain in her life as a nun with her community or to seek dispensation from her vows and face life alone. Sr. Mary was mature, having already lived many years as a nun and a teacher. But she had suffered a breakdown and was sent to a therapeutic community for persons in religious life where she felt nurtured and valued in a way she never had experienced. Unfortunately, her year in this supportive community ended. She was not ready to return to her religious community. She had to learn to live on her own for the first time in her life with no community to guide her. She found herself living in a tiny apartment in the city, working with computers. Her father had just died.

Our long tumultuous relationship began, transforming both of us in the process. Over the next few months, she cried, raged, blamed, confided in me and gave me a glimpse into the trauma of a child who felt worthless and abandoned. Her father was not as perfect as she had described him. He sometimes drank, which had made her mother cry. Mary was called at a young age to do God's will, so she became a nun. Her father had told her that because of her sacrifice he would go to heaven.

As a therapist, I believe timing is crucial, and knowing when to wait or hold one's tongue is essential in therapy. Over many years my aim and timing have improved. I owe much of my early progress to Mary. Whatever advantage I gained as the therapist was matched by Mary's emotional neediness and constant sparring with me. Yet we grew to respect each other deeply, especially our faith lives. My feelings about Mary—what psychoanalysis calls counter-transference—had a good workout during those years. Her perception of me bounced back and forth from admiration to devaluation as her emotions tumbled out from fear to hopelessness, and rage to tenderness. I followed as best as I could, even the day she enacted her own "death" scene as she recalled the times she lay on the floor as a child when her mother ignored and stepped over her. Most of the time I kept my feelings locked inside. Mary showed me what feelings look like in all their colors. There were days I lost my cool and responded back to her taunts. Next session she would begin by talking about my responses! Most of the time, I was surprised to realize I had helped her. Unlike her mother, I was able to accept her feelings and celebrate her aliveness.

I became the captain of her team, connecting the dots between her gentlemanly and caring psychiatrist, her beloved surgeon who cured her of breast cancer and helped her grow in trust, and a Sister from the Archdiocese of Boston who assisted her in reconnecting with her own community.

A more practical or intellectual counselor might not have understood the full impact of her needing to keep her vows. Yes, the vows connected her to her father, an authority complex, as well as to abandonment and emotional abuse, but here was also a person who committed her life to a faith community, and the core of her identity and authenticity remained there.

I continued to have some intense exchanges with clients. One day I asked Cherie, an African-American client, if she had ever felt anger toward me. She certainly had reason to express rage at the abandonment and abuse she experienced as a child. Her process was different though; she took it out on herself by cutting and withdrawing. Her response to my question was, "No." She smiled shyly. "You are gentle, like a deer to me, like my grandmother."

Did I underestimate the fragility of intimacy with women who suffered both abuse and racism? Not as well as I wished I had. Perhaps our time and connection were enough, as not all therapy takes place in linear time or solely during the encounter of two persons sitting across from each other. Often I would not see the fruits of the seeds that were planted. But one afternoon several years later, I participated as clergy in an Ecumenical Service at the Fall River Catholic Cathedral, and there was Cherie singing in a Gospel Choir. We embraced, celebrating with pride her voice, her joy. These encounters were the color of the heart: precious, tender, and unforgettable.

SEVENTEEN

Catholic Meets Protestant

What you do matters—but not much. What you are matters tremendously.
—Catherine Doherty, *Madonna House Staff Letter #140*

I WAS DETERMINED TO REMAIN A CATHOLIC WOMAN SEEKING JUSTICE AND knowledge, not set apart by the community for a special purpose, but eager to meet the world out of my own faithful conscience. During my first weeks of seminary, I was often asked the identity question: What are you? To my surprise it meant what type of Christian are you, or what denomination do you belong to? The Boston ethnicity question was not being asked: Roman Catholic, not Italian. Our freshman class at Andover-Newton was equally split between women and men. The two largest denominations were United Church of Christ (Congregational) and American Baptists, the seminary's founding groups, followed by Roman Catholics and Methodists.

The diversity of religious backgrounds and persons with differing perspectives opened me to an expansive, inclusive faith. Medieval Church History was taught by Rev. Dr. Eleanor McLaughlin, an

Episcopal priest. Ellie, in her round glasses and tight curly brown hair, appeared to embody the seriousness of the Anglican Church tradition with a rather funky personal rhythm. Watching her rush into class in her running shoes while donning her black clerical collar with a bright t-shirt over it delighted me.

At that time, Catholic women in seminary knew a job would not be forthcoming in ministry. Yet we went to seminary totally engaged in study, in awe of the possibility of Divine Providence, committed to doing our part to create justice in our churches and the world. In many ways the eighties were a heady time for women to be in seminary in the presence of prophetic, gifted theologians, ethicists, and pastoral leaders who fought repressive structures in church and society but also served and ministered to us seminarians and to their religious communities.

One day Ellie led a service in the student lounge, a room with dark woodwork and upholstered chairs. She put on her priestly garment, slowly and reverently explaining its significance: "First I have an alb, short for *tunica alba*, a white tunic, because that is the color of Jesus's grave clothes, the color of the angels' clothes, and thus the color of the resurrection." Then she took a long, white rope. "This is a cincture. Jesus told Peter that when he was old, someone would tie him with a belt and take him where he did not want to go. The stole is the work cloth that slaves wore around their necks. It is the yoke of Christ that one takes on at ordination as a servant of Christ."

Through Ellie's gestures, "priest" became both demystified and mystified. In a simple, intimate way, she told us the story of what priesthood meant for her.

My story began to take root in my soul. I wrote: "A Church transformed will come about when Christians let go of dead images and begin to image the consciousness of Christ. To do this we will have to take responsibility for our lives of faith. It is time that we stop asking permission to do what is right and good. Instead of asking the Church to be, let us be the Church."

My comfort level was about to be challenged. Since I was enrolled in a master of divinity degree program, even with no hope of ordination as a Catholic female, I would need to fulfill a field education placement. Outside the field education office, the school posted profiles of Protestant churches looking for a student intern. Initially, I was skeptical, not being able to picture myself in a Protestant church, but a faculty member, seemingly unaware how this might be problematic for me, encouraged me to set up a couple of interviews. One interview took place in a small upper room. Three Presbyterian elders in dark suits with dour expressions quizzed me, "Do you have a personal relationship with Jesus Christ?"

"Uhh," I said.

"Do you know about the walk to Emmaus in Scripture?"

"Emmaus? Please, a clue?" I thought to myself, never good at remembering names.

I knew I wasn't ready to jump into a Protestant milieu! It still felt foreign to me, especially sitting with these conservative elders. Had I been able to interview with a more liberal Protestant parish that was sympathetic to my Catholic background and my interest in social justice and feminism, it could have had a different outcome. My theology could not be reduced to a systematic formula. Later I would elect process theology and study the liberation theologies, including feminist theology. Moreover, my gift primarily was pastoral, guiding each person to a deeper, fuller appreciation of God's enlivening presence. As I came to understand the Emmaus walk, we are always in the presence of Jesus, the Divine One, but it isn't always apparent to us. God's mystery draws us through our faith and willingness to be attentive. Like Jacob, we come to realize that God is in this place, and we never knew it.

My discomfort with the elders led me to return to the field education office to search deeper into their files. Reaching as far back as I could in the dark cabinet, I unearthed a yellow file with the words, Ministry, Spirituality, and Changing Life Styles.

I read excitedly: "This project is designed to enable participants to gain understanding and develop ministerial skills in the midst of changing lifestyles and relationships: students will be expected to become involved in task work of their design and/or pastoral counseling under supervision, human growth workshops in holistic and spirituality settings."

Regrettably, this project was defunct. However, I contacted and persuaded the director, Rev. Dr. Calvin Turley, to take me on privately to design a group called Alternatives in Spirituality and to receive pastoral counseling supervision for my work at Healthsigns. Cal was a Diplomate in the American Association of Pastoral Counselors (AAPC), the highest-ranking certification for the profession.

Immediately, I felt at home in Cal Turley's presence. We met in his office at the Swedenborg School of Religion. The school was a spacious brick mansion in a residential area in Newton. Cal's office was small, heavy with dark woodwork, and stuffed with his books and papers. He reminded me of a character out of a Dickens novel with spectacles, a round reddish face, white sideburns, and soft blue eyes. Though his movements seemed slow and plodding, I sensed some impatience, even a touch of gruffness that suggested to me that the world was annoying him in some way.

We got along so well that I continued to meet with him after my one-year field education commitment. His approach to psychotherapy and his integration of psychology and religion inspired me and helped me with my pastoral counseling formation. There came a day, though, when I too annoyed him. I had spent half a year in one of the groups he led on scripture and our personal pilgrimages. The group consisted of Swedenborgian seminary students and recovering alcoholics from Cal's practice. When I don't feel safe in a group I withdraw and feel bored, wanting to belong and be involved but not finding an authentic way to connect. I decided I couldn't continue being uncomfortable for one more semester as time always felt so precious to me.

Cal was upstairs at the school in a huge room cluttered with books and papers and many wooden desks of other staff. There were no dividers. It felt weird compared to the tight intimate space of Cal's office. Timidly, feeling exposed, I approached him. "I can't be in the group next semester. I have other courses and work I need to focus on."

Cal got very red in the face and blasted me, "You can't just stop now. You need to go back and try it again. It will be different this time. Someday you will be older and you will have many responsibilities. You can't just quit."

I persisted though shaken by his anger. I hit a nerve. Later in the year I felt vindicated when Cal invited me back to process with his colleague the strengths and weaknesses of that group. He talked about subgroups and how this group contained three subgroups: theological students, members of a recovery group, and one supervisee (me). Two of these groups were acquainted with each other. I was in a group by myself, which made me feel like an outsider, which I was. As time went on, group leadership became a specialty of mine. I learned how to build trust and take care to welcome everyone's participation. I knew what it was like to feel excluded and uncomfortable.

The group I designed, Alternatives in Spirituality, met in my apartment. I recruited gay women who were seeking empowerment, spiritual growth, and coming out support. I valued the process of discerning when to guide the group and when to let the participants shape the discussion. We told our stories, we named our demons, and talked about ways to dispel the power they held over our lives. At the end of the evening we had a ritual with candles and incense; each person read their "demon" aloud. As each woman burned her list in the fire, a liberating energy filled the room. When I spoke, I looked to see the glow on their faces as they met my eyes. Growing up in a church where rituals were connected with authority and authority with God, none of us could experience our own power. Yet these rituals gave life.

Back at Andover-Newton I had a very stimulating academic year. I was part of the Catholics on Campus group, facilitated by faculty member Dr. Maria Harris, a former Catholic Sister of St. Joseph who taught religious education reframed as "religiously educating." Maria, a renowned author in Catholic circles, was as wonderful a person as she was a teacher. Her course was interactive, artistic, and playful. She assigned us the book *Interplay* by Catholic theologian and former priest Gabriel Moran, whom she later wed after returning to her native New York. *Interplay* formed the foundation of the course in which we explored four aspects of life: work, community, education, and Sabbath. Our assignment was to write a paper on one of the four aspects. My choice of Sabbath was easy as I valued sacred space. *The Sabbath,* by Rabbi Abraham Heschel, filled my longing for the sacred as a "palace in time." Heschel wrote: "The art of keeping the seventh day is the art of painting on the canvas of time. . . What is so precious to captivate the hearts? It is because the seventh day is a mine where spirit's precious metal can be found with which to construct the palace in time, a dimension in which the human is at home with the divine."

Maria, too, was pioneering as the first Catholic full professor in the seminary. She facilitated Catholics on Campus, a group that met monthly in the formal Berkeley Room under paintings of past presidents of Andover-Newton, all male, looking down on us. Ten of us sat on settees and armchairs, sharing our experiences about our studies, our personal lives, and what it meant to be Catholic in a Protestant seminary.

"Do you remember the time when both popes died within a month?" Maria asked us. "Do you know," she said, incredulously, "I had some colleagues approach me offering their sincere sympathy, and I even received sympathy cards!"

"They still think the Pope controls us?" we roared, laughing.

An appropriate time to send a sympathy card would have been when beloved Pope John XXIII died. The Second Vatican Council that he assembled made it possible for Catholics today to benefit from the ecumenical transformations evidenced by us sitting in the Berkeley Room at Andover-Newton! The subsequent backlash and reactionary direction of the Roman Catholic Church are worth many sympathy cards.

Judy often came with me to the group meeting and attended events on ethics, faith, and contemporary issues. She got to know and love Maria too. Maria declared gleefully, "We should give Judy an honorary degree."

Still, Judy felt awkward in groups, which caused her to talk off the top of her head while trying to fit in. One night during check-in time, she blurted out, "Maria, I thought of you the other day when I saw the headline in the *Boston Globe*: 'The Pope declares masturbation is a sin.'"

Silence. Then Maria burst out laughing.

My Catholic dilemma would not be solved during freshman year of seminary. While I thought my life in seminary was moving in a Good Orderly Direction—Julia Cameron's metaphor for call—I was unprepared for what lay ahead.

EIGHTEEN

Sorrows Past and Present

You prepare for one sorrow,
But another comes.
It is not like the weather,
You cannot brace yourself,
The unreadiness is all.

—Derek Walcott, "Odd Job: A Bull Terrier"

O when the Saints go marchin' in. O when the Saints go marchin' in. Lord, I want
to be in that number . . . The bouncy organ drew us out of our shock and grief.
We filed out into the bright sun from the tiny Swedenborg Chapel near
the Harvard campus. From a distance I spotted my pastoral counseling
professor, Dr. Merle Jordan. I wished I might run and catch up to him, but
I had no words, no sense but to keep on walking away into the June sun.

Cal, my mentor, had died.

Judy and I had been invited to move into Cal's office building and
collaborate with him on developing a holistic health and counseling center. While we were moving boxes into his office, my friend Richard York
approached us with the news that Cal had died in Maine while on retreat
at his cottage for a weekend of renewal. How could this be?

Cal died. Judy and I looked at each other, incredulous. We had seen
him just a few days before. Cal had been worried about himself but pre-
tended to be fine. He told us he hadn't felt well that very morning and
drove himself to the hospital where he was told to get a stress test and
then quickly released. Judy became concerned and had made him promise to get the stress test as soon as possible. We put aside our worry and
continued to make our best laid plans.

Cal died. Judy was filled with remorse. "I should have been more
insistent," she said. "I didn't come on as strongly as I should have. Now,
it is too late."

Cal died and with him our hopes for a new beginning to work toward
the integration of psychology and theology with the support of a man I
loved and respected. It would have been a gift to make up for other losses
and barriers: my father's death, the Catholic Church, the oppression of
gays. I was deeply disappointed and angry.

Cal died. How dare he die! Why couldn't he take care of himself?
Why did he spread himself so thin? Here he was, yelling at me: "Someday
you'll be a workaholic like me." If only we could have designed our holistic practice, made a new life for ourselves.

Cal is gone. Now I must forge a different path, reinvent myself once again.

＊

Cal's sudden death brought back memories of my early encounters with death. In the summer of 1962, after fourth grade ended, Johnny and I were on Cape Cod for the weekend with my father's brother Uncle Philly's family. The first anniversary of my grandmother's death was only days away. My father's mother, whom we called "MaMa," was quiet, with deep-set eyes. My mother told me that MaMa seemed serious because her first-born son died in the influenza epidemic of 1919. My father, only fourteen at the time, rushed out in desperation to find a doctor, but no one came in time to their home in Roxbury. My grandmother went blind from grief; she prayed, bargaining with God that if she regained her sight, she would never do handwork again. She did regain her sight and indeed no longer did the delicate needlework she had learned as a child in Italy.

I felt good being with MaMa. When I was sick with an ear infection, she came and heated something on the stove, using her knowledge of herbs to cure me. She taught me to play *scopa*, an Italian card game. I felt overjoyed whenever I got the magic card, *settebello* (seven of diamonds), in my hand.

When I was eight years old, MaMa was in her late eighties. One day my mother told me my grandmother had suffered a stroke. She and my other aunts took turns tending her at my godparents' house. I can remember solemnly going up to her bedroom. The large gray flowered wallpaper frightened me as did seeing my grandmother bedridden. MaMa smiled to put me at ease. I don't recall exchanging any words; my mother said MaMa spoke only Italian after the stroke. We hoped she might recover, but she had a fall and soon died.

My grandmother's wake and funeral took place at my godparents' home on Anawan Ave. One memory remains from that warm day in July. I stood on the front porch with my daddy who was talking with his brother Uncle Willie. I was glad to meet my uncle, who had married and remained in Germany after serving as a cook in WWII. He had sent me my first transistor radio in a brown leather case. Uncle Willie was warm and sweet; my mother said that of all the Ierardi boys, he was most like my father. I stood on my father's brown shoes with patterned perforations on them as he swayed me back and forth on the front porch.

Back on Cape Cod at Uncle Philly's, I heard the phone ring. Johnny was called to the phone. After the call he walked out to the living room where I was sitting. He looked out the front door into the sun. The faraway look in his blue eyes could not disguise the desolate, dispirited, and disbelieving change that had befallen him. I knew something was terribly wrong.

My brother left to return home in his car just as another car arrived for me. My older male cousins on my mother's side of the family were recruited to bring me to Aunt Helen's in Dorchester. How odd to have cousins from the Verrochi side of the family arrive. I sat silent in the back seat as my cousins conversed with each other. An hour and a half later we arrived at my aunt's house. The next moment my aunt rushed me out the back door as I threw up my breakfast all over the concrete steps. During the next couple of days, ordinary life mimicked the usual school vacation weeks with my cousins Bobby, Paula, and Janice. We walked to the movies, the zoo, and watched *The Flintstones* on TV. Everyone was extra nice. In this land of make-believe and incongruities, I listened for voices in the night from the master bedroom as I strained to make sense of what was happening.

One morning my mother appeared dressed totally in black. I was dressed in an orange matched shorts set. My tanned back felt bony, strong, and taut. Standing over my mother, for the first time I saw her large full body in mourning as she sat on the edge of an upholstered chair facing me.

"Daddy died," she said, trying to hold back her tears. My bones drew me in tighter and tighter. I stood silent like a soldier. My mother didn't usually expect responses to her pronouncements. This time was different.

"You must have known something after you got sick. Did you know?"

I denied knowing, both needing my mother and not wanting her near. I wanted nobody. Who could I ever trust again? She gave me and my cousins all the change from my father's pockets then left me until after the funeral.

My father loved to make adults and children smile. My cousin Julie recalls how he kept an account for the cousins at the local candy store. My father was the only one in my family who didn't appear to tower over me. He was small in stature, possessing a quality of gentleness evident in a yellowed black and white photo in which he carefully leads me, age two, down the wooden stairs of our front porch on Willow Street. I recall him singing Brahms's "Lullaby" to me and calling me the apple of his eye. Each night Daddy tucked me into bed, saying prayers and wishing me sweet dreams.

My father worked as an electrician. Born in 1906 in the early days of electric lights, he wired his large family home in Roxbury. Though my mother's usual stance, coming from her strong Abruzzese roots in the mountains of central Italy, was "hard work never hurt anybody," I think she was troubled by the stress of the physical work he did. Years later, my brother Johnny, in a rare moment of candor, said that my father spent Saturdays working, visiting his parents, or food shopping. He regretted not having had enough time with him. I liked accompanying Daddy on Saturdays, whether it was shopping at the stalls in Faneuil Hall or watching him fix relatives' lights. I remember when he took me into the Chancery building in Boston. I grasped the sacredness of the place looking through the stained-glass windows.

In another photo of my father and me at the Franklin Park Zoo, he is bending over, handing me peanuts to feed the goats, llamas, and ponies. Pigeons flew over my head at the zoo, frightening me as we walked along the uneven pavement. The presence of birds felt ominous. I had a large fairy tale picture book that I spent hours wandering through before I could read, anticipating with fear and excitement the page with a huge bald eagle, beady eyes bulging, deadly talons hanging. I'd quickly glance then turn away as I do now when a poor little critter is hit on the Cape roads.

Going into fifth grade with Miss Hardy was a blur except for the time we made Father's Day cards, and she said it was OK to make one for another man in our lives. I made one for my godfather. I went out to the corridor to get some water to paint with at the large black soapstone sink. My former fourth-grade teacher, Miss Sullivan, approached me. A fleeting image went through my mind of her opening the high windows in her classroom with a wooden pole, belting out the tune "Everything's Coming Up Roses!" I only turned partially toward her as she said gently, "I am sorry to hear of your father's death." Feeling awkward and embarrassed yet grateful she noticed and cared, I muttered something in reply.

The last time I saw Miss Sullivan was at her wedding. My mother brought me to Holy Name Church, the church where I was baptized, the church with the large apse with Christ the Good Shepherd in the middle and all the sheep encircling him. Holy Name Church is an imposing basilica in the Romanesque Italian style. When we moved to the other side of West Roxbury, we attended a more modest white wooden church, St. John's Chrysostom, a church my father loved for its simplicity. But I missed the sheep and the sense of majesty and mystery.

My mother and I climbed the monumental stone steps to the entrance of the basilica. My mother was dressed completely in black as it was still within a year of my father's death. She knew I loved Miss Sullivan, so she escorted me to the wedding ceremony. We sat in a back pew. When my teacher saw us as she came down the aisle, she smiled with tears in her eyes.

Embracing me, she turned toward my mother saying: "Mrs. Ierardi, I am so touched that you have come at this time."

NINETEEN

Across the Charles

The very contradictions in my life are in some
ways signs of God's mercy to me.

—Thomas Merton, *Faith and Violence*

ENTERING MY SECOND YEAR OF SEMINARY, I CROSSED THE CHARLES RIVER
to matriculate at the Episcopal Divinity School. The dean of admissions
remarked to me wryly that the differences between denominations were a
matter of manners. This I pondered. Did he mean the difference between
Anglican and Catholic? I did come to adopt certain manners at EDS. After
evening prayer in the chapel, all were invited for a glass of sherry at
Tyler Hall, a Tudor-styled room with a large round stained-glass window.
Each month Dean Guthrie and his wife invited Judy and me to dinner
at the refectory as part of the EDS community. We appreciated their
hospitality. In 1984 Judy was considered a "spouse equivalent," a step
up from "significant other." Episcopalians are renowned for the proper
naming of all manner of things from titles to rooms.

There were oddities I encountered at EDS. I was referred to as a
"Roman." As the only Catholic in the master of divinity class, I guess "Roman" could have meant Italian Catholic. My Aunt Portia, who had been
an Italian professor, believed we were descended from the Etruscans. My
friend Kyriaki FitzGerald, a Greek theologian, insisted Ierardi is Greek
meaning "of the holy."

Another delightful oddity at EDS was a flower garden endowed by
a lady in the vicinity who loved walking on campus. Every couple of
months, the gardener completely changed the flowering plants to keep
them looking fresh and appealing. Each day at lunchtime a plentiful bowl
of cottage cheese was placed on a long wooden table in the refectory, also
endowed. I learned to like, not love, cottage cheese.

I loved being at EDS. The progressive curriculum allowed me the
flexibility I needed for my course of study. As a Roman Catholic woman,
ordination was not going to happen for me.

The Boston Theological Institute, a consortium of nine theological
schools, offered the riches of many traditions, theologies, and teachers.
Once enrolled in one of the nine seminaries, I could take fifty percent
of my courses in any of the other schools. Since I knew the city so well,
I chose courses at five of the schools: Andover-Newton, Boston College,
Boston University, Episcopal Divinity, and Harvard Divinity. Under-
graduate experiences at Lutheran and Catholic colleges had prepared me

well. I believed ecumenical education shaped me not only for the sake of learning but for the sake of healing the broken Body of Christ.

In a predominantly Episcopalian setting, I needed to examine my beliefs and practices. One day when I felt conflicted about such a mix of religious identities, a seminary classmate said to me, "How fortunate will be those you work with as you have been able to tap the riches of many traditions, such as the spirituality and theology of Catholics and the hymns and biblical studies of Protestants." Looking back, God was giving me the confidence I needed through the generosity of my encounters with others.

The anchor for my time at EDS was Curriculum Conference. This group's purpose was vocational formation as well as designing our curriculum for the master of divinity degree. Each week we met at the apartment of Rev. Dr. David Siegenthaler, priest and professor of Church history. While David's "manner" and tradition were solidly Episcopalian, his large heart accommodated our unconventional group. Jim, a senior student, co-facilitated with David. Jim, a bright, intense man with thick long dark hair that fell over his forehead described himself as a poet and a Marxist Christian; he was about to be ordained as a priest. Later I learned he had a congenital deformity that in time would worsen; I believe that added to his sense of urgency about life, which I could relate to, adoring his intense manner and magnanimous heart.

Each week, four of us entered David's apartment in a large stately faculty house on Brattle Street. Professors Sue Hiatt and Carter Heyward also had their lodgings there. Both would become important mentors to me at the school. Large ceilings and windows let in plenty of light; modern furniture with comfortable couches added to our welcome and ease for the intimate conversations and explorations ahead of us.

Our first task was to write and share a paper on our spiritual journeys. Barbara, a quirky woman with blonde hair and quick speech, plunged in: "I was raised in the South, in Virginia. I have two young children, and I hope there is a place in this school for a mother with children. My husband, Jim, and I are astronomers. There has to be a place where science meets religion! That will be my calling, my project: faith and science." Looking at me, she said passionately but with humor: "I don't mind, Anne, that you're a lesbian. But an astrologer!"

Wilma, a thin, short, brown-haired woman, laughed. "Yes, and here I am a psychic! I started out a skeptic, an agnostic until I began having these experiences many years ago of other worlds. I wrote two books under a pen name. Eventually, I realized I was called to minister and counsel. I love the ritual and communion in the Episcopal Church. However, when I met with the Bishop's Council, they didn't care to hear about my faith. Instead they had read my books and focused on my 'irregular' past. I left discouraged."

Wasonga, a priest from Kenya, exhibited a quiet strength, focused on the "now," the present time. One day Jim told us that as he walked past the flower garden, he spotted Wasonga sitting on the stone wall that bordered the flowers. With tears in his eyes, Jim said, "Wasonga was singing to the flowers." Wasonga talked about reaching out to young people in Kenya. At home, he went wherever he felt a need, even to a bar to share the gospel in his simple and loving way. If he ever felt judgmental or uncomfortable about our North American privilege and self-absorption, he did not let on.

I remember our group with great affection and the skillful caring way that David and Jim mentored and accepted us. Each of us had a unique struggle finding a home for ourselves in the church but we were buttressed by the love and respect we showed for each other.

As I grew inwardly, I felt it was time to make a deeper commitment by choosing a spiritual director. When Jim told us he would be providing direction at the Monastery of St. John the Evangelist near campus, I approached him. requesting direction. He smiled his generous smile and said yes!

TWENTY

Les Jolies Roses

Throw your dreams into space like a kite, and you do not know what it will bring back, a new life, a new friend, a new love, a new country.

—*The Diary of Anaïs Nin, 1944–1947*

DRIVING UP TO THE PARISH RECTORY, THE FIRST PERSON I SAW WAS LOUIS, THE caretaker. With rich dark skin and a broad smile lighting up his entire face, he welcomed me to my field education site at St. Luke's Roman Catholic Church. Like most of the congregation, he had emigrated from Haiti. When I emerged into the bright sunlight after meeting Father Bob in the rectory, I was delighted to realize that Louis had washed my Buick. I waited with him while the sun dried the car.

Louis was a refugee. I celebrated Louis as Person of the Month in the first parish newsletter that I designed. We talked about the parables Jesus used in the gospels. He spoke about the parables as being hard to understand initially: "Until the Spirit comes to enlighten."

He compared his parish to a cemetery where all are received: *Tout le monde est benvenu sans distinction de race, de couleur et de religion.* ("Everyone is welcome regardless of race, color, or religion.") His gardens *de jolies roses* he dedicated to *La Vierge Marie*.

A few days later when I moved my car closer to the old convent, I noticed the door of my car was smashed in on the driver's side. Someone had backed into it from a driveway. I felt upset and sad not just for what had happened but that it happened during my first week. I felt less safe. What a contrast to Louis's ministering to me as he washed my car just as Christ had washed his disciples' feet before his arrest. Over the summer, material things that we prize in "better neighborhoods" faded into the essential goodness of the people. I was welcomed into parish life.

A Haitian Institute, a week-long workshop, took place at St. Luke's. Mornings we studied Creole, and evenings we learned about the history, politics, culture, and religion of Haiti. I was amazed at the resiliency of the Haitian people and appalled by their history of oppression by Papa Doc as well as the profound disparity between our country and their island. In the seventies people continued to leave Haiti. Our professor commented, "The Haitian government encourages people to leave . . . they don't welcome the deportees back. The real term is flight not emigration. They are leaving a country where there is no political or economic hope. This is an historical problem."

In the second week Judy and I attended Mass spoken in several languages, including French, Creole, English, and Spanish. We heard wonderful music sung in French and Creole and participated in a procession to celebrate the Feast of Corpus Christi. Although I didn't understand all the words, I felt the mood—simple yet grand. The irony was that the Irish-American pastor knew less of the language of the Mass than the people of the congregation. Fortunately, Father Bob, the other priest, and Sister Claire came from French backgrounds and communicated well with their parishioners.

Parish ministry was busy and I cherished contemplative moments. Just sitting in the rectory sipping a cup of tea around a large oval table brought me peace. Fr. Bob was always running about. One day he returned from the Boston Food Bank with a van full of food that we stocked on the pantry shelves. Later we picked up a group of nine children, brought them to the rectory to practice singing with my guitar, jumped back into the van to visit a nursing home where the kids distributed drawings for the residents. The next week Sr. Claire brought me with her on home visits. I felt despair at seeing the living conditions and the struggle of the people. They had so little. So much I took for granted. Behind the church, an arsonist had set fires to the homes of forty-one people. The next day we took five boys to Nantasket Beach. Weather was fierce: rain, thunder. The water was freezing. Yet the boys were having a grand time, soaking in every moment with pleasure.

Fr. Bob tried his best to give me a good experience at St. Luke's. He especially hoped I would preach, as Sr. Claire often did. He believed it was good for the congregation to see a woman on the altar giving the Sunday sermon. I was so afraid. I wrote synopses of scripture for the Sunday bulletin, but I regret to say I never preached. At the time I believed I would get out of seminary without preaching because my goal was pastoral counseling. In a year's time that would prove false.

Unfortunately, an unhealthy tension grew between Fr. Bob and me. I also sensed discord in the rectory. Was it between Sr. Claire and Fr. Bob or maybe between them and the younger pastor? I couldn't tell, but my distrust of my mentor grew. The last day, Fr. Bob withheld his final evaluation from me until he was sure I would finish the parish newsletter. I was smug, secretly angry that he didn't think enough of me to trust that I would never leave without completing the newsletter, my final contribution to the parish.

I left Fr. Bob's office after finishing the newsletter and returned to the kitchen. Louis looked so sad that I was leaving. Then he started cooking. Quickly, the staff and several parishioners appeared to send me off with drumming and other joyful instruments. They presented me a mug of red roses with "Anne" printed on it.

A few years later I ran into Bob and Claire at an ecumenical event. They were married. Both had served the church for over twenty-five years. Bittersweet. *J'ai deux amours* ("I have two loves"). Two precious loves that could not be reconciled. Not in the Catholic Church. What a loss to the people. Many years later, I read in the *Boston Globe* that the younger pastor had been accused of sexual abuse.

[top] Marching with American Baptists at Gay Pride in San Francisco [bottom]
My Baptism at Walden Pond

Gay Rites

The Third Call: 1984–88

There seemed no easy way out.... First, I had to face my underlying fear: Did I have enough inner courage to seek ordination? Looking back, I would add, did I have the fortitude as a gay Christian with artistic leanings to hold my own in the face of the ecclesiastical powers and outmoded traditions that still permeated all churches?

[top] Chaplains at Worcester State Hospital [middle] Seminary graduation: (l–r)Uncle Connie, Aunty Rosie "Angel," me, my mother [bottom] "The Three Sisters": My mother, Aunty Rose, and Aunty Lena

TWENTY-ONE

Chapel Week: Fall

We begin to realize that God moves among us, transcending our particularities. She is born and embodied in our midst. She is ground and figure, power and person, this creative Spirit, root of our common life and of our most intensely personal longings.

—Carter Heyward

IN THE FALL OF MY SENIOR YEAR, I PULLED A NOTE OUT OF MY MAILBOX. With the official seminary heading, I saw it was from Dean Guthrie: "As a senior member of the master of divinity class at the Episcopal Divinity school, we invite you to assist in a week of chapel services, including Morning Prayer and Eucharist."

The Episcopal Church had endorsed women's ordination only about ten years earlier. Rev. Carter Heyward and Rev. Suzanne Hiatt, professors at the school, were two of the original eleven priests who had challenged the tradition of ordaining only males to the priesthood. While the Church declared their 1973 ordinations to be irregular, the following year they were recognized, and a door that was closed for centuries opened at last. I knew about Carter before I came to EDS, astonished and moved by her cutting edge book on being a lesbian and a priest. I met Sue when she interviewed me for admission. Sue and Carter were ever-present to me by their witness. Their courage and prophetic voice entered the deep cavities of my heart.

An invitation to assist at chapel! I took this in, trembling with anticipation. Me, in vestments standing on the altar?

An Italian-American classmate, formerly Catholic, was preparing for the priesthood at EDS. She often appeared when I needed a push. One evening I was invited to a dorm party. For some reason, I didn't have a bra with me that day and felt self-conscious. My friend said, "If you have it, flaunt it." I later found out she had had a mastectomy.

When I shared my doubts about accepting the dean's invitation as I was the only non-Episcopalian in my class, she counseled me to "go for it!" And so I did. My friends Ann and Ellie offered me a place in their room to sleep as most of my services would be at 8 a.m. for Morning Prayer. I didn't own any vestments. The school loaned me a black cassock. A short priest who worked in administration lent me his white surplice to put over the cassock. I was all set to go. Marvelously, I learned that the priest in charge would be Sue Hiatt! God must really be serious.

I woke up early, anticipating the watershed moment of joining Rev. Sue Hiatt at Morning Prayer in the beautiful chapel. It all seemed unreal. I was entering a liminal space, a dimension of body and soul that had not been possible for me as a Catholic woman. Entering seminary three years ago, I knew I was called. At the time I thought I could define the call. But soon I realized it is not entirely up to me as God is leading me to a new place. Here I am, Lord. Show me.

Sue was larger than life, humble, steady, righteous. I can't remember a word she ever said to me, but her presence has never left me. Becoming a minister of God began that day as we stood in the awesome St. John's Chapel, she on one side of the altar and I on the other. I showed up. God did the rest.

Later that week Judy and I attended Mass at the Paulist Center. I reflected in my dark red sketch book: *Sexism is the biggest obstacle.* In his homily about leadership in the Church, the priest called leaders to humility and service. It hit me how masculine his viewpoint. Women naturally serve and are humble, often socialized to be that way, but what about feeling courageous and proud, claiming the authority that is rightfully theirs in the church? Serving in chapel services helped me break through my barrier of denial and doubt: "If God is for us, who can be against us?" (Romans 8:31 NIV) Three days later, I wrote: *There's a poignancy in the air now; when I stop to gather a breath I feel a sweetness—a liberating presence.*

Yes, I am called to some kind of ordained ministry. Where, when, what, and how were still unknown. I clung to my favorite Bible passage: "For now we see only a reflection as in a mirror; then we shall see face to face. Now I know in part; then I shall know fully, even as I am fully known." (1 Corinthians 13:12 NIV)

I wore a t-shirt that I brought back from a conference in St. Louis. It was tan with a large black figure of a woman holding a chalice above her head with the words, "Called to a Priestly Ministry." At that conference Roman Catholic women had gathered from all parts of the country to name and celebrate our call to be priests in a renewed priesthood— priesthood based on authentic calls to ministry and justice unrelated to sex and gender. I met several women from the Midwest who were active in their parishes, already living out a priestly ministry without being recognized by the hierarchy. On the plane returning to Providence, I sat with Annie Milhaven, a high-spirited, fearless, witty woman theologian, originally from Ireland. Annie introduced me as the next Catholic bishop to the gentleman seated next to us on the aisle seat. What a hoot she was to be with! I love these brave-hearted bright women who stay in the Catholic Church to fight. Little by little, although I would remain connected to Catholic feminists and social justice groups supporting the Women's Ordination Conference until the day when ordination has no gender, I was coming to feel that my calling was elsewhere.

I began to realize that I had to find my own way into a ministry I would be most suited to. My calling as a pastoral counselor was leading me to focus on God's mystery, one person at a time; to see Christ in everyone; and to be led in prophetic ways to heal God's people. I discerned God didn't really care what denomination I was in. What mattered more was who I was becoming and how fully I could exercise my gifts.

TWENTY-TWO

Chrysalis: Winter

We know then that joy is the sweetness of contact with the love
of God, that affliction is the wound of this same contact when it is
painful, and that only the contact matters, not the manner of it.

—Simone Weil, *Waiting for God*

AFTER CHAPEL WEEK, I COULD NO LONGER BE CATHOLIC WITH A BIG C. God was calling me to something beyond what I understood. I felt I wasn't ready to be ordained in a Protestant denomination.

There seemed no easy way out. A real puzzlement like a Zen koan. It seemed so unfair. A heavy burden for me to take on. Or was it all up to me? What else could I do? The only way through seemed to be to persist in journeying through this maze of uncertainty. God knows She instilled in me a large dose of perseverance. Perseverance and impatience—a real fun combination!

First, I had to face my underlying fear: Did I have enough inner courage to seek ordination? Looking back, I would add, did I have the fortitude as a gay Christian with artistic leanings to hold my own against the ecclesiastical powers and outmoded traditions that still permeated all Churches?

My senior year advisor at the Episcopal Divinity School was a former Catholic nun, Bessie Chambers. Her spiritual advice to me was "wade in the water" until the right path unfolds. She was certain it would. So, too, was a classmate who reminded me every time she breezed past me on her way to class: "I'm praying for you! I know it will happen."

Realizing the enormity of this peculiar calling to ordained ministry that still honored the internal changes occurring in me, I decided the time had come to consult a therapist. Since I was studying pastoral counseling, it would become necessary for my professional formation. Even though my reasoning was sound, I felt anxious and afraid. Judy had already begun seeing a spiritual director, Sr. Marie Doyle. Marie recommended a psychologist, Dr. Patricia Papernow.

On the appointed day, I walked into an old, tall Victorian-style house. It could have been a set for a Hollywood horror movie. My imagination was getting the best of me. I walked in and sat in a narrow corridor by a very steep staircase. When the therapist was ready, she called down to me from the top of the stairs. I climbed up the stairs, hanging on to the old banister until I arrived in a long narrow attic room. "Enter through the narrow gate. For wide is the gate and broad is the road that leads to destruction, and many enter through it. But small is the gate and narrow the road that leads to life, and only a few find it." (Matthew 7:13 NIV)

Attics held mysteries for me. From my early guitar years with Mr. Mulcahy to my Emmanuel years in the art department with Sr. Vincent, attics had become a place of initiation. I sat down on the edge of the couch in the therapy room. As much as was possible, I let her talk. I came to learn this was a good therapy tactic. Get the therapist to do most of the talking and eventually she may do the emoting too!

Even though I knew she was there, I felt heavy, out of my body, like a hanging dam. She was lively, friendly, and attentive, so unlike the psychologist I had worked with briefly at the Menninger Foundation whose distance heightened my ability to disappear. I tried to keep my cool composure, keeping my thoughts close to my chest. Her initial comment, the first interpretation, may have been only meant as an observation, but I experienced it as confrontational, even intrusive: "Do you always talk in headlines? 'The President Arrives' . . . then what?"

I grasped the humor, recoiling. Having older brothers who enjoyed teasing, I knew what it felt like to laugh while feeling angry inside.

This process hurt. Wow, I can't believe I am doing this—am I crazy? I grew anxious experiencing the wildness inside in the presence of someone intent on psychic surgery. Is this what the Catholics describe as limbo or is it purgatory? My energy had nowhere to go. I wanted to flee, but the overwhelming reaction was spacing-out, fog, going nowhere. For several sessions we sat in long gaps of silence with Pat asking, "Where are you? Where did you go?"

One day Judy said to me as I was trying to analyze my dilemma: "Is the meaning you derive from an interaction always dependent on your self-worth?" I was speechless. Another koan. *A puzzlement*, as I could see Yul Brenner exclaim with his finger in the air in *The King and I*.

Meanwhile, Pat was getting closer. I felt grateful for her presence even though a wall existed between us. She asked me to "act out" the wall. The wall was long and huge and was constructed a very long time ago. I felt a mist enveloping me in sadness. I confessed to her, "I don't object to your poking at me." She replied, "I am in a bind because I hear you saying to me, 'come closer' and 'fuck you.' I wish I didn't have to work so hard."

Too bad, I think.

Therapy is rather a curious combination of confession, meditation, writing morning pages, being in love. It is funny and sad, happy and mad, hiding and seeking. Therapy is making room for yourself and in that room a place to experiment, to relax, to go around in circles until you reach the center.

One day I brought slides of my paintings to share with Pat. I imagined I was still holding some cards to my chest and I desired to show my hand, one at a time.

"Your paintings are bold, expressive, and filled with color. I can feel you through them. The world is impoverished by not seeing you."

Yes, I thought, my paintings soar like birds in the air for they have no fear; they are joyful. They are free. Might that be the real me?

Being with Pat over the years must have been like Georgia O'Keeffe meeting Stieglitz or Gertrude meeting Alice B. Toklas, having someone who knows and supports you and invites you into the world once hostile and cold. How rare in a world often lacking grace, mercy, or justice.

I wrote a poem contrasting the Incarnation, Jesus as the Word of God with "no thing" in Zen Buddhism. My early interest in Buddhism and Zen meditation had drawn me to a place of emptiness and letting go. Yet I struggled to embody within myself my identity and belonging to my own Judeo-Christian faith.

I brought this poem to Pat to share my increased capacity and desire for mutuality:

I chose a simple faith, a God who was destroyed
and not a God my mind achieved: one distant, non-disclosing
as Chinese mountains would they fade should I go to touch them.
This God brought you to make me feel the "I" that I was missing
So I could taste and speak the joys before my thoughts erased them.
Then I would bear the fruit of mutuality,
and you could taste and hear and touch the beauty that is me.

Likewise, authentic talk therapy is not about words either. These words, at their best, become incarnate and embodied. Deep therapy occurs when the soul connects with body and a new self emerges like a butterfly. In the words of Jungian author Marion Woodman, "that is what going into the chrysalis is all about—undergoing a metamorphosis in order one day to stand up and say I am."

TWENTY-THREE

Preaching as Divine Activity: Spring

Wade in the water
Wade in the water, children
God is gonna trouble these waters

—African American Spiritual

AS MY CLASSMATES PREPARED FOR GRADUATION AND ORDINATION, I STILL waded in the water. I had avoided a class on preaching until my last semester in seminary. I dreaded public speaking. However, I knew I must study with Professor Cannon. Besides, her course Preaching on Ethical Issues concerned the writing of sermons, not delivering them in class.

The Holy Spirit appeared in the person of Katie Geneva Cannon to trouble the waters, to find a way where there was no way to make me a preacher, not only by following her rigorous instruction from the Black tradition but also by embodying the Word made flesh in Jesus. In other words, I could not do the work of composing a sermon without becoming changed. Dr. Cannon instilled in me how to tell the awesome story of God's glory embodied in the Word as the most serious and the most sacred work one can aspire to.

The seating in class was graduated stadium-style. From my safe perch toward the back, I could see Professor Cannon way down below, a perfect view. How to describe my teacher and mentor? She appeared strong, self-possessed, personable but not personal. I think she wore an Afro in those days. Her warm, expressive, convicted voice is what remains in my mind. A woman of prayer, her faith shone through the aliveness of her teaching. I knew that life had not served her on any silver plate of social privilege whether through church, race, gender, or academy. I knew her words to be true and she gained my trust. It must have been the power of the Lord. What else would move me in such a way that I too would be surrounded by God's grace. She opened each class with the words:

God, we pray that you'd show us the way.
Show us the way not to fortune nor fame,
nor to win laurels or praise for our name,
but show us the way to tell the great story,
to live the great story.
And thine is the Kingdom and the Power and Glory. Amen.

Georgia O'Keeffe painted flowers larger than life so they could be seen. Dr. Cannon knew the tremendous responsibility that God's ministers have to the people. I feared being mature enough to stand on the altar of God, but through Katie and other women who guided me, I could become one who would tell the great story.

> 'Tis Grace that taught
> My heart to fear
> And Grace my fears relieved

Dr. Cannon never said anything she didn't believe and didn't practice herself: "I have to believe in what it means that the Word is Incarnate, and therefore I proclaim it from a place of authority. I proclaim it with some conviction . . . I can't preach what I don't know."

She taught, "Preaching is divine activity whereby the Word of God is proclaimed related to a contemporary issue. Every sermon is a call to live more faithfully. And the congregation that hears has an opportunity to say, 'yes I will,' or 'no I won't.' There's no lukewarmness in preaching. You can either drive them into the hands of the Lord or further into the arms of the devil!"

Now, as a Catholic, I knew divine activity was happening in the breaking of the bread, in the Eucharist. But here, every week, Katie proclaimed God's presence among us: "The Word of God is Jesus Christ incarnate. And part of what happens in the divine activity is that the Word becomes flesh in the preaching . . . There is no holier thing than to proclaim, 'Thus said the Lord.' And if I can make, in every sermon, God present to the people, I have done what I have been called to do."

Now I could receive the power of preaching as the Word made flesh embodying the essence of grace, a Divine experience of communion. Here was the bridge to cross from Catholic to Protestant. I followed Professor Cannon's rigorous instruction "writing" sermons that she marked as "excellent."

Do the work your soul must have.

—Katie Geneva Cannon

Rev. Dr. Katie Cannon was the first African American woman to be ordained in the Presbyterian Church. I learned later she was so ahead of her time that there wasn't even a ceremony to recognize her. She wrote a book on preaching as divine activity modeled on the teachings of Dr. Isaac Clark, who taught her and many African-American pastors over decades. He didn't want her in his class as she was a female, and he believed women did not have anything of substance to say. But she proved herself to him. "That was the challenge I needed," she said.

Katie knew what it was like to struggle against adversity. When she was twelve, she worked alongside her aunt as a domestic in a wealthy white household. Raised in North Carolina in a mill town in the 1950s, a black woman's only work option was cleaning homes for Whites. One day, she told us, "I was frying chicken when the household buzzed me to wait on them. The chicken fat was splattering in my eyes and my skin was burning. I cried out to my aunt that I needed to stop. My aunt handed me a stick of butter to soothe my skin and told me to keep on frying. I said to myself that day, 'My life had to be different no matter what it would cost me. I didn't want to have to work with my face on fire.'"

I recall my own teenage years the summers I worked alongside my aunt in a hospital. Aunty Irene and I prepared dietary meals for kidney patients. The dietitian in charge paraded us into her office every morning, checking our legs for panty hose and our hair for hairnets. While she was a "Mrs.," she addressed us by our first names. The permanent help were middle-aged, gray-haired, faithful women from Boston neighborhoods. The large, well-dressed, blonde-haired dietitian was much younger from an upper-class family in New York. We easily saw through her demeaning attitude laced with a false nicety. She patrolled the kitchen to make sure we wouldn't eat a morsel of the food we cooked. One day, tempted by the smell of cinnamon rolls hot out of the oven, we gave in. As my coworker, an African American girl who missed her home in South Carolina, was about to take her last bite, Mrs. Dietitian turned the corner into the kitchen. She tossed her roll into the cabinet as we looked at each other trying not to laugh with our mouths full. The defiance of that simple act of eating was worth the danger.

TWENTY-FOUR

Gay Rites: Summer

Whenever we speak the truths of our lives in situations of which our truths are unwelcome, we are like intense light, difficult for others to bear.

—Carter Heyward, *Touching Our Strength*

After graduation from EDS I attended friends' ordinations and installations in their new parishes where they could now bring their gifts to ministry. I envied friends entering through the front door with all the ecclesiastical recognition and celebration of the completion of their seminary training.

June approached along with Gay Pride Week in Boston. That year an event caught my eye: Gay Rites, a panel of LGBT religious leaders were to speak of their struggles in their faith communities. I grew excited and then disappointed. Excited to see and hear persons of faith and courage speak out but disappointed to grasp the depth of pain and exclusion. Of the dozen or so leaders, only one pastor, Rev. Monica Styron, had come out to her congregation. The others remained in the closet for fear of losing their jobs, which they undoubtedly would have. I couldn't wait to visit Rev. Monica's church, which we did the first Sunday after I heard her speak.

Old Cambridge Baptist Church was plainly decorated and worn due to congregants moved more by peace and justice work than by building maintenance. It had great gothic arches and beautiful original Tiffany stained-glass windows in the parish hall where years before I had danced with Jocelyn through "The Joy of Movement."

In the middle of the service, people in the congregation stood up to tell a joy or concern: "I was on Storrow Drive and I ran out of gas and Marty happened to be driving by and helped me." "My buddy John is dying of AIDS. It is a horrible disease." "I am moving on Saturday. Would the OCBC mover's club (whoever was available from church that day) help me?"

Rev. Monica preached on a passage from the book of Isaiah: "I have called you by name and you are precious in my sight." (Isaiah 43:1, NRSV) During the sermon she called out names of her congregants as she looked at us from the pulpit.

I heard her say, "Anne."

Did I really hear that?

The prophet Isaiah spoke to me through a woman, a gay woman, like myself. She knew firsthand the hurt of being different and having to struggle for a place in the church that excludes so many. Could I believe in a new heaven and a new earth based on God's love for me?

Monica's sermons came from her own experience. She understood how we had disguised and erased our existence. Instead of knowing that we are created in the image of God, we had become something else. Our healing happens through asking and through petitioning. Healing begins by asking on our own behalf. Monica was telling me that God desires and responds to all of me, the real me, which is what liberation theologies are all about.

I had been erased. I erased personal pronouns. I erased the "who, what, where," of the body. I had to STOP erasing so I could conceive and execute boldly the image of me created by God in goodness.

This precious year of formation opened the way to fully embrace myself as a person and a budding minister. The interweaving of Old Cambridge Baptist Church, therapy, spiritual direction, and seminary provided the perfect meal prepared just for me at God's banquet!

TWENTY-FIVE

Revolutionary Integrity

Stay dreamers who act and move toward a vision. Each day do something. We are the earth, people! Let's be about it!

—Sr. Marjorie Tuite, OP, talk given in Los Angeles, 1986

I FLEW OUT TO LOS ANGELES FOR A QUICK SUMMER VACATION BEFORE MY doctoral program started. While Johnny was the one family member I spoke to freely about myself, I also grew angry with him. I no longer liked being a kid sister, but he was ever the elder brother, teasing me, setting the agenda. He liked to tell people I was really his older sister! Gay men have to be forever young while lesbians take themselves too seriously—as women we felt we had to. He really irritated me when he called me Theresa—my mother's name. When was he going to grow up or, as Theresa would say, act his age?

Los Angeles was never restful, though I enjoyed Korea Town and its cave-like spa, the Bodhi Tree bookstore, the best Belgian waffles on Sunset Boulevard, film studio visits, and Hollywood parties. Waiting for Johnny so I could get a ride to my friend's church on Sunday frustrated me. Letting on might invite more teasing. Being a master of deflection and evasion, Johnny rose late after watching double-featured classic Hollywood movies, then sat at the breakfast table in his bathrobe with his long hairy legs crossed, and chatted on the phone with friends and business associates. Suddenly he would dress, rush out, jump into his red convertible curse the freeway traffic, and arrive late for his destination. Gemini!

That week I discovered there was a conference of feminist nuns at USC. I felt fortunate to be welcomed to their amazing leadership, inspiration, and community.

Sr. Marge Tuite, a great Catholic activist, was a keynote presenter. A massive woman, soulfulness emanated from her like shooting stars that I wanted to catch. Marge predicted accurately that things would worsen in the Catholic Church. She preached we had to stop "going on vacation" and face reality. She called us to "revolutionary integrity." "Seeking ordination," she said, "in the Roman Catholic Church as it is today lacks revolutionary integrity."

I came to realize the enigma of Catholic vs. Protestant was not essential to the path before me. While we all enjoyed learning from each other and experiencing each other's traditions, the bigger picture for me was finding a place in a church where neither I nor anyone would need to erase or be erased, a place where all our gifts would be honored.

My calling gradually centered on the three big I's: integrity, inclusion and integration. Living into my integrity proved challenging as I had already discovered when I applied to schools for doctoral work. I had placed two applications: one to Andover-Newton and the other to Boston University. I was accepted at Boston University. Then one afternoon I received a call from the pastoral counseling department at Andover-Newton.

"Hello, Anne. We have your application for the Doctor of Minister degree. We would love for you to come here, but we have a policy that you have to be 'endorsed' by your denomination before you graduate. Since you are Catholic, you cannot be endorsed unless you are a priest or a nun. I see from your admissions essay that you are considering transferring to another denomination. You are welcome to start in September, provided you change denominations."

I already knew in my heart my days in the Catholic Church were limited, but I detested being discriminated against. I knew of the discriminatory policy of the American Association of Pastoral Counselors (AAPC) who would not endorse lay Catholics. I knew it was wrong so I wanted to challenge it. I preferred to go to a smaller seminary like Andover-Newton, but I believed I would be lacking in "revolutionary integrity" if I accepted and changed denominations just to get in. I went to BU. The policy at Andover-Newton eventually was changed.

Looking back, I can see that while my soul was rooted in European Catholicism, my mind had a strong American Protestant spirit. During my three years of seminary, I intentionally chose courses that would yield a well-rounded knowledge of both Catholic and Protestant Christianity, perhaps unconsciously trying to heal this historic rupture in western Christianity. I studied with women, both Protestant and Catholic, who were pioneers of feminist and liberation theology. My Bible professors were Protestant while my theology professors were Catholic. I studied Sacramental Theology with Jesuit Bernard Cooke at Boston College where I met an older nun in a modified habit, Sr. Mary Katherine.

One day while we walked together after class she asked, "Do you believe in Divine Providence?" I replied with ease, "Surely it must be so." I brought her to see Andover-Newton. As we walked through the campus, she laughed and said I would never make it as a religious, especially when it came to obedience. Judy and I took her to our favorite restaurant in Chinatown. Having a nun in the car got us a parking place right in front of the Lucky Dragon. "I am an adventurous eater," she said. A year later we spent a couple days with her at her convent in Pennsylvania. Just being with her my spirit and body relaxed, and I felt at home.

While the Catholic religious life as a priest would not be a road open to me, the presence of many Catholics leading and nurturing me cleared a path in my wilderness faith journey. One day a card appeared in my mailbox with a return address of "Bishop McAtee." Imagining a very revered note from a church authority, I carefully opened it, discovering it was from a couple I knew through Healthsigns. The card had an ecclesiastical border of reds and greens. It said: "If, after all, one cannot always make history have a meaning, one can always act so that their own lives have one." These words by Albert Camus became my mantra, bringing me wise counsel to go where I would be led in the moment, allowing direction to come from the Holy Spirit, trusting that "all will be well." I framed their card and kept it on my wall for many years.

My discernment process finally had ended. Ultimately, I chose to act so my life would have meaning. I came to the clear decision that I would complete my pastoral counseling training and apply for full membership in the American Association of Pastoral Counselors. While I had loved attending Mass at the Paulist Center, I realized there was no one to miss me if I left. I began to feel more love and inclusion in the intimate community at Old Cambridge Baptist Church. I wanted a place where the whole of me could belong.

When I told my stepfather I was becoming a Baptist, his immediate response was: "Italians are practical people. I hope you don't take this the wrong way, but will it help you get a job?" The Italian immigrant speaks!

Yes, there would be losses, misunderstandings, and challenges. But I needed to move forward, to share with people who would benefit from my gifts. I took the next step, moving on toward a doctorate in pastoral counseling and carving out a place for myself as a woman in ministry.

TWENTY-SIX

Worcester

The ward is like a circus of naked human chaos. I used to paint this, but Christ, don't give it to me in the flesh! Who am I here? As chaplain maybe I'm the negative (the empty) space in their lives as compared to the other professionals. And so I'm here to learn; the patients can teach me if I present myself as teachable. Who then is this gift that is me, in the flesh, in this circus of naked human chaos?

—Author's journal, first week at Worcester State Hospital, 1986

As part of my path to become a pastoral counselor, I had to complete a unit of Clinical Pastoral Education (CPE) in the summer. I applied to one Boston general hospital. The interviewer opined, "I am not concerned that you wouldn't be present with a patient who is dying but that you wouldn't bring your feelings back to the group." It is true that I was partly concealed. In those days I needed to remain closeted. It was dangerous to be "out" in ministry, so I tried to avoid situations that might be harmful. CPE supervisors often acted provocatively to confront seminarians. I finally decided upon a placement in a psychiatric hospital, Worcester State Hospital.

At our hospital orientation, the medical staff prepared us for the worst. They shared a threatening statistic that one out of five people ended up in a psychiatric hospital. I wondered if that might have been true "in the heyday of Worcester State" but today more people end up homeless or simply untreated.

Even though we wore chaplaincy badges and spent a couple of hours a day on the wards, our main training aimed to prepare us psychologically for the ministry. Toward that end, each week we wrote verbatims, dialogues of our experiences on the wards. CPE was like group therapy for ministers. At the end of each afternoon we gathered back in Tom's office for "group dynamics." Our supervisor, Rev. Tom Sullivan, while a kind and gentle Episcopalian priest, seemed to be lying in wait for our issues to emerge. We were a quiet group; only one of us, Marjorie, was comfortably articulate. One particular afternoon, none of us wanted to initiate a conversation. Since I too shared the awkwardness in the group and was an expert at holding silence, I rather liked the challenge. We held silence the whole time. Finally, the hour was over and Tom dismissed us, unwilling to rescue us.

As chaplains we struggled with how to make meaning out of suffering and how to bring hope where there was despair. In order to understand the patient as a human being and understand our own felt experience of the patient, our training emphasized being over doing, observing over directing, feeling over analyzing. The wards were sparsely furnished, like a prison. Chaplains, unlike doctors, nurses, and aides, wandered the halls and sat among the patients, usually in the day room. Our only task was to be there and later to reflect and write about our experiences. We also took turns conducting a weekly prayer service.

I grabbed the opportunity that summer to learn more about psychiatry, especially object relations psychotherapy. Each week included fantastic lecturers who came to us from the faculty at Worcester State and the University of Massachusetts next door. I borrowed many of Tom's books, including writings on therapy by Karen Horney and Harry Stack Sullivan. I read the fascinating autobiography of Anton Boisen, *Out of the Depths*. Boisen was the founder of CPE and the first Chaplain at Worcester State Hospital in 1924. Boisen had in fact been committed to an institution for a mental breakdown. He wrote, "as individuals come face to face with the ultimate realities of life and death, religion and theology tend to come alive."

After a few weeks I wrote in my journal: "A chaplain is engaged in a struggle with life, death, and meaning. The chaplain has a 'calling.' She engages with the will of God and her own desires, moving and protesting toward God on behalf of those she ministers to, giving hope and seeking clarity where there is confusion. A chaplain, most of all, is a 'wounded healer,' who, knowing both joy and pain, can accept and support healing in others."

My assignment placed me in two locked wards. Unlike the patients, I held the key. They warned us to open the door quickly as there may be a patient preparing an escape. One day as I pushed open the heavy steel door, Lucy lunged toward me and said with her clipped voice, "It is the Chaplain." In her early fifties, Lucy had wavy blondish brown hair, wore square glasses and a bright, flowered smock. She amused me. I wanted to get to know her better. She was usually moody or belligerent and spoke with a cynical, clipped style of speech common in the Boston neighborhood where she grew up. The previous week, as a morning group meeting for patients had gathered, she had distanced herself, moving quickly down the corridor with her arms held rigidly behind her, looked back and mocked, "You are all a bunch of co-co-nuts." Today, however, she gave me a full smile. I invited her outside for a drink and a chat even though I was always a bit nervous leaving the ward.

The next day I got permission to take a woman named Kathy to the Catholic chapel. According to her chart she was homeless, referred to Worcester through the court system. She had lost her mother a year ago and was showing assaultive and regressive symptoms. Her diagnosis was borderline and dependent personality disorder. I filed all that information in the back burner of my active mind because at this moment I wanted to encounter her person-to-person.

Kathy had asked me a few times to bring her to the Chapel. When I entered the ward I was happy to see her dressed with a maroon blouse and dark blue slacks. She was dancing briefly with a male patient to rock and roll. She appeared playful and awake, unlike me who arrived tired, silently praying as I walked down the corridor to be present, open, and caring.

Honestly though, as we walked to the chapel, I felt worried. It was my first time leaving the ward with a patient for a religious purpose. The small chapel was adorned with holy statues. I sat diagonally in back of Kathy. She described how her mother neglected her and also did not let her keep her children. I expressed empathy but also needed to redirect her to prayer and away from a meltdown. I wrote in my weekly verbatim to my supervisor, Tom, in the format required:

Chaplain (me): "Can you give these worries to God? Can you put them in God's hands?"

Kathy: "God, I put my worries in your hands. (Kathy moves intently into prayer.) That you will take care of those who are hurting: the Jews and Arabs, the Holocaust, people in concentration camps. Vengeance is mine says the Lord (Oops—getting angry I record). They'll be punished, people on drugs, with diseases, people without teeth."

Chaplain: "Can you trust that God hears you and will decide about judgment?" I ask quietly.

(Tom wrote in the margins of my verbatim: "The words about vengeance got the chaplain anxious.")

I was indeed apprehensive saying the name of God, invoking the power of God's name in this holy temple. But as I let out my breath, speaking the name of God, prayer began.

Kathy: "I put it in your hands God, I pray for people who are alone, who want a partner, I need a partner (crying). Why can't I have a husband and children like other people? (Looking right at me.) I didn't think I would get so sad."

I acknowledged her sadness. I was sad too. Suddenly she became worried and paranoid, talking about people who were watching her and talking about herself as a child.

Chaplain: "Do you know the Bible verse about the lilies of the field?"

She replied to my amazement:

Kathy: "They don't worry about what to eat and what clothes to wear. The lilies neither spin nor work. I always liked that."

Chaplain: "And God protects and loves them," I respond with tenderness.

Kathy: "Yes, God does." she replied softly.

I am moved by the special privilege of witnessing Kathy's prayer. We were both affected and became relaxed in this sacred space. I tried to act as a guide while keeping the wolves of stress and paranoia at bay for a precious while. She guided me into prayer at the end, something I confessed to Tom I was not confident about, praying freely and earnestly as Baptists do.

Chaplain: "Would you like me to say a prayer?" Kathy nodded in approval. "Dear God, I believe that you have been with us today, that you are interested and attentive to Kathy's prayers and concerns. We pray that you will give her peace of mind and freedom from worries. We thank you for being here with us and for loving us just the way we are." (Tom wrote affirmatively in the margin: "Sounds like a Baptist.")

For some reason, the wards were organized geographically by towns in central Massachusetts, not by type of patient or diagnosis. One day a tall, thin, confused, elderly woman I had never seen before came over to where I was sitting in the day room. She lunged at me and grabbed my arm. The chess player who usually sat silent playing in the corner of the room, diagnosed with schizophrenia, suddenly rushed over and pulled her away from me. He and I had hardly ever conversed, but we connected in that moment. I was ever grateful to him after that, always nodding hello to him when I saw him on the ward.

Another request from the nurse's station to see a minister came from June. The chart said she cut herself in the abdomen to gain admission and now showed regressive behavior, refused to eat, and was unable to leave the hospital. June led me to her dorm room and laid down on her bed. Her body was covered with red sores; her hair cropped short with a thick growth of hair on her chin. She reminded me of a waif from *Oliver Twist*. She said in a sad whiny voice: "I haven't eaten for one month. They gave me an enema and made me drink fluids. They are killing me." She pulled up her dress and said, "See, this isn't human. They are going to put me out on the streets and bury me alive."

I was embarrassed and probably afraid to look at her body. When I did I saw a pale, wrinkled, depleted body. Please give me the strength to not run out of the room, I begged God!

"Look at me; I'm a vegetable. Tell me, is this human?"

Did I believe that this is human? What, within me, could say yes. God, this vision of what a human being could become was terrifying! Suddenly erupting in me, power emerged out of weakness, and I found my voice.

"Yes, June. You are human like I am human."

She stopped for a second, looked at me questioningly. "You think so?"

"Yes. I do."

We continued talking. She kept raising her dress, telling me that nothing would stay down. I thought to myself, what am I going to do now? Should I stick with the goals of the team to try to encourage her to accept treatment? Should I see if she has any spiritual concerns? Should I pray? I decided to try all three.

"June, do you think there is anything you could do to help yourself?"

"It's too late (whiny but strong). I should have never taken the enema. They are trying to kill me. I shouldn't have listened to them and now (yelling desperately) what am I going to do?"

"You seem to feel like it's hopeless, which makes it hard for us to help you."

"What am I going to do? It's too late. I can't even die with the body I have."

"Do you believe you can ask God to help you?"

"No. God deserted me long ago. He left me by the road."

"June, you asked to see a minister. How about if I say a prayer before I leave, and I'll come by and see you tomorrow?" She cried and continued to show me her abdomen. When I prayed she grew quiet.

I returned to the nurses' station. The nurse showed me in her chart that all the medication, including penicillin for her infected sores that were self-inflicted, had been refused. The diagnosis read: "factitious disorder" and "dependent personality." What a combination! There was nothing physically wrong with her. I had never seen such desperation. She laid in bed all day, sometimes in a fetal position. Where was grace or hope or sin here? Was it my hope that told her I promised to return tomorrow? Was it hope that made her ask for a minister, or was I just one more person to complain to, to get sucked into her needs? Did she even have free will? Was this illness something created by God or by the devil? Does life get so unbearable for some people that they can only cope by negating and destroying themselves while crying for someone to nurture them?

I did return the next day. I surprised myself by being very persuasive. I told her to make "bite-sized" goals (no pun intended). I gestured the amount with my fingers and asked her to do a little at a time. I visited the next day and saw she had liquids by her bed and was even dressed. I told her she was looking better and supported her taking in liquids. She tried to deny that it was doing any good. I ignored her complaints, focusing on her strengths. I was delighted to see she was more connected with me, feeling a sense of relationship. Even though June was the patient who challenged me, she toppled my notions of human nature. Perhaps I knew that June and I were not that different.

The next day I peeked in to find she was under the covers asleep in her fetal position. I returned the following day to hear her complain that she ate a peanut butter sandwich and it wouldn't digest. I myself had never been able to digest peanut butter sandwiches, so I could truly empathize.

"If you had been here yesterday, you could have helped me," she said accusingly.

I defended myself, "I did look in, but you were sleeping."

"No, I wasn't asleep."

Glenda, a patient who befriended June, walked by and talked to June affectionately but firmly. June tried to frustrate her attempts. Glenda reached out her hand and lovingly tapped June saying: "What you need is a kick in the pants."

I continued to visit June. I thought about my identity as artist and now chaplain, how hard I had worked at bringing beauty and hope together to transform ugliness and the pain of being human. Transformation was the hope, the vision of something new. Perhaps this time I was seeing creation raw without a clear sense of transformation. Perhaps there were no answers here but there was a kind of "rest" here. A time of Sabbath, of letting go and letting God take over.

What happened to June? I don't know. Outcomes were not part of being chaplain at Worcester State. Being present to the patients and to ourselves was the challenge. Meditation in action. Faith without guarantees. As the year went on I carried June in my soul; she touched me and changed me. For a short time in her life, I visited her every day.

Day after day at Worcester State I saw the nakedness of human pain amidst glimpses of the beauty of humanity and kindness. What remained when all the trappings were removed from ourselves?

A new psychiatrist appeared at the hospital, a poised and perceptive older Austrian woman. She saw me drawing one day outside the building. Coming closer she said, "If you can do that, why are you here?"

I couldn't answer her directly. I realized I wasn't sure myself. As time went on I came to know that being an artist was also about being, feeling, observing, and understanding what it was to be a human being, even if it required the better part of a lifetime. The two disciplines become inseparable.

Meanwhile, I was still ill at ease with my CPE peer group, more so than on the wards. Only Tom knew I was gay. At thirty-two I was by far the youngest in the group. Charlie and Helen were retired science teachers. Helen was an Episcopal lay woman; Charlie was a Catholic deacon who had raised a family, but since his wife had died, the Roman Catholic Church allowed him to become a priest. Jerry was an older Irish Catholic priest with an artistic bent in the midst of a mid-life crisis. Marjorie was a middle-aged Catholic lay person, sharp and intellectual. We were an odd bunch with a lot of life experience, not the usual seminarians.

Marjorie and I were sharing a house nearby, provided to us by a church organist who was away for the summer. Marjorie was an intimidating woman. Her manner of speech, her intellectual knowledge, and her sarcasm felt dangerous. Given my amiable nature and listening skills, we got along well enough, though I was never really at ease, especially during the first few weeks. Marjorie liked to have a beer after a long day at the hospital. She talked incessantly about "object relations theory." A lot of it was over my head, but I was determined to understand her fascinating theories.

I chose to focus on object relations in my doctoral program. Robert Fox became a mentor and champion. His teaching and supervision, the Institute for Existential Psychoanalytic Object Relations Therapy, would intrigue and challenge me, grounding me in a philosophical and authentic way to enhance my work with clients. What once seemed too abstract became clear and integral to understanding the deeper struggles within myself and the people who sought my help.

I often felt emotionally spent, longing to have Judy to come home to. Hiding was also doing a job on my emotions, especially as my days were so intense at Worcester State. My moment of truth arrived at dinner one evening. Marjorie, in her English accent, said, "When are you going to share with us your beautiful homosexual relationship?" I nearly choked on my dinner. After that dinner conversation I came out to the group. Their acceptance lightened my concerns and left me much freer to appreciate their companionship. I was grateful for Marjorie's words.

Marjorie and Jerry, the Catholic priest, provided the most drama in our group dynamics, rather protecting the rest of us quiet ones from having to open up too much. Unfortunately for Jerry, he represented to Marjorie all that was parochial and dysfunctional about the Catholic Church. I shared her rage at the church that passed over people like her and me, intelligent Catholics who would never have a place at the table because of our gender. The intense anger Marjorie directed at Jerry took my breath away as he tried to wiggle out of his Roman collar. Father Jerry was a product of the Irish Catholic Church in Boston. I saw both his privilege and his limitations. If priests were treated like gods, it was their humanity that suffered. Jerry reminded me of a large teddy bear that was put into a cage too young and never could find a way out. I felt compassion toward him and have often wondered what became of him after our summer. I believed at heart that he was an artist and that he would have made a good actor. One day he impersonated the church ladies in his parish, pulling out his handkerchief and dusting off the wooden chair saying, "O Father, sit down . . ."

Toward the end of our summer, Tom assigned each of us another member of the group to write a pastoral life history about. I was to write about Jerry. I suggested to Jerry that we go out to the Sticky Wicket Restaurant in Hopkinton. We could relax and enjoy the Dixieland music and he could share his story with me. I wrote:

What distinguishes Jerry is his bearing and posture. He moves from immobility and rigid comportment to creative gesturing with a red, lit-up, smiling countenance. His speech moves from quiet, obedient, priestly intonation to light-hearted spontaneous mischievousness.

He was raised in a Protestant town near Boston during the post-Depression era. His father died when Jerry was a teenager, and his mother had to work to support the family. After thirty years in the parish, Jerry reached a personal crisis leading him to get help in a therapeutic community. He went on to study expressive therapies.

Jerry saw himself as a man torn between the life he had lived and the life he might have desired. He had sacrificed so many of his desires and ideals to convention, family, and church that it had become hard for him to envision his spontaneity and joyousness as something that need not be experienced alone.

My report ended with this recommendation for the Catholic Church:

The church could have understood him more as a person and less as a function. They could have recognized his talents in the arts, for example, and let him integrate these gifts in his ministry.

Deacon Charlie interviewed me and wrote:

I saw Anne as cool and shy and I was put off by her. After spending time with her in preparing this history, I have found her to be a bright, warm, and sensitive person who has suffered much in her search for self-identity. I find her charming and outgoing and a person of strength and love for people. She knows who she is and where she wants to go. She knows what she wants to do with her life.

CPE ended with a dinner party at Tom Sullivan's antique home. Our group posed for a final black and white photo at the foot of the steps to the imposing façade of Worcester State Hospital.

TWENTY-SEVEN

The Heidi House

This is your body, your greatest gift, pregnant with wisdom you do not hear, grief you thought was forgotten, and joy you have never known.

—Marion Woodman, *Coming Home to Myself*

After that intensive summer of CPE, I returned to Judy and our home in Roslindale, back in the neighborhood, still waiting, as I waded in the waters of God's call. I found solace and precious space at an enchanted place of healing I named the Heidi House. Heidi came on the recommendation of a Catholic sister from Boston Catholic Women who was helped by Heidi's touch as she healed from breast cancer. After dialing Heidi's number, her voice brought a smile to my face as I heard her bright sing-song southern German accent: "Hello, this is Hei . . di. Hope your day is filled with much happiness."

Climbing the steps to Heidi's apartment on the second floor, I seemed to no longer be in Boston. Instead, an enchanted village of body, mind, and spirit rose before me. Her house appeared as a typical two-family, dark-brown dwelling like the one I grew up in. The traditional, quiet, mostly Irish Catholic neighborhood had changed slowly over the years as newcomers moved in from different places. After Heidi buzzed me in, I walked up two flights of stairs past a mythical green gnome on her landing.

Once inside, time stopped. Heidi lived on body-and-soul time rather than clock time, what theologians call *kairos* time. Our ritual began with a cup of tea sitting on colorful Indian pillows. Her home was filled with mythical and mystical mobiles twirling from the ceiling, bright hangings, and Oriental tapestries. She invited me to talk about my life in the present—my joys and concerns. Then Heidi, wearing her spacious flowered dress sailed into her little bathroom to prepare my tub . . . just for me!

Trained in the great spas of Germany, she chose the right herbal solution from a collection of Dr. Kneipp's colored bottles. He had become famous in European spas as a Swiss herbalist and physician. There was red rosemary for energy, green eucalyptus for the cold season, and yellow melissa for stress. Heidi had a portable whirlpool attached to her porcelain tub. Before long, I began to unwind as I watched the bubbles move in whirling rhythm. Was this a dream? I smiled inside. Wasn't this the best kept secret in my old boring hometown? Maybe Heidi needs a boarder. As Judy Garland told her fans when she played the Palladium, "I'll just stay here and never go back."

Heidi returned with a huge white towel. She took my thin-boned hand into her fleshy strong hands and guided me out of the tub. She dried my back while I dried my front. Then she escorted my naked body into her massage room that was just large enough to contain the table and Heidi. I climbed up and immediately let Heidi take over. No need to tell her where I hurt; she already knew where to knead my body in her masterful yet gentle way. She smoothed out the worried lines on my forehead.

After the massage, we returned to her living room with her hanging mobiles and yogi quotes, and sipped more tea. Heidi sent me on my way with a warm hug and kiss. She was born under the sign of Cancer, symbolic of the Great Mother, embracing all of life and loving unconditionally.

One night I dreamed that Heidi was my landlord, and I went upstairs and cried in her arms. Next day I felt peaceful, finally experiencing a hiatus from my hectic days.

A few years later, Heidi closed up shop and moved to Amherst to an assisted living facility. Her aging body could no longer perform strenuous body work. I purchased a plethora of Dr. Kneipp's oils to use when soaking in my own tub in the evenings, dreaming of the enchanted Heidi House.

TWENTY-EIGHT

Walden

Nothing is far and nothing is near, if one desires...There is only one big thing—desire. And before it, when it is big, all is little.

—Willa Cather, *The Song of the Lark*

At Old Cambridge Baptist Church, every person seeking membership appeared before the deacons not only to request they join the church but to share what led them to their decision. The deacons wanted to listen to each person's faith stories in their own words. For gay folks joining the church, this could be a deeply moving experience. One gay man described to me how his father, a pastor, suspected he had an attraction to his childhood friend and made the boys come into the sanctuary to hear the father preach against homosexuality. He was so bruised by this experience that he still had a hard time sitting in the church facing the cross. Rev. Monica joined him in the pew to help ameliorate this early trauma.

I shared my feelings about becoming a member:

To seek and then to find is a part of our faith journeys. We look not only for a place to stay and rest, but we look also for a place where we can be found. We usually are aware of our wanderings and our seeking but not often aware that we are also being sought. In the darkness we meet our aloneness, our fears, our emptiness. We learn the truth about ourselves in time. If we turn around we may see the search lights of God looking to be with us. And God looks in many ways—witness the many flashlights in this congregation.

I asked the deacons and the pastor if I might receive Believer's Baptism. They were surprised at my request given I was already baptized. Most Protestants—unlike Catholics who claim seven sacraments—recognize only two sacraments: Baptism and Communion. Baptists often hold a dedication ceremony for a baby but baptism customarily occurs when a child is mature enough to understand their relationship to Christ—typically in early adolescence.

When I told a seminary friend, an Episcopalian, that I would receive Believer's Baptism, she said, "You can't be re-baptized because you were already baptized as an infant." I said I wasn't being "re-baptized" because I believed that ritual is not a static thing that is done once and for all. Ritual symbolizes our growth in relationship to God, a sign of what God is doing in our lives and in our faith community. My first baptism was my birthright as part of my family and parish. For many years, I had felt caught in a tension between adaptation and creation—following convention or following one's creative call.

This second baptism became my mature response to a God who respected my desire for authenticity, the God who asked "Who do you say that I am?" I asked the deacons to hold my baptism at Walden Pond in Concord, a special place that had dwelled in my imagination since reading Thoreau as a teenager in my backyard one hot summer's day. Walden represented a sense of freedom of the soul and finding one's quiet place in the natural world. It also signified my place as a New Englander, a lover of philosophy and literature.

In preparation for my baptism, I practiced swimming in the waters to lose my fear of going underwater. Friends and church members gathered on the rocks above the pond. They sang, accompanied by guitar, "Shall we gather by the river?" Thoreau's closing passage to Walden Pond was expressively read by Rev. Cindy Maybeck:

The life in us is like the water in the river. It may rise this year higher than man has ever known it, and flood the parched uplands; even this may be the eventful year, which will drown out all our muskrats... such is the character of that morrow which mere lapse of time can never make to dawn. The light which puts out our eyes is darkness to us. Only that day dawns to which we are awake. There is more day to dawn. The sun is but a morning star.

Then Monica and I, dressed in white robes, entered the water. She pulled me back into her arms and dunked me and brought me back up again. The waters sparkled with holiness. This was finally the end of wading and the beginning of immersion in a new life within a community of seekers at Old Cambridge Baptist Church. It was also the beginning of a new chapter in my life that would take me to some hard and often lonely places.

Now that I had received "the right hand of fellowship" in the Baptist Church on Easter and received Believer's Baptism in the summer, I applied for Watch Care, the American Baptist Church process for ordination. I was assigned a Watch Care pastor, Rev. Dan Buttry, who guided me through the process at our meetings in his church, Dorchester Temple. Marty Hackett, a deacon and nurse midwife to the Chinese community in Boston, became an inspiration, modeling for me the hallmarks of progressive Baptist values: faithfulness through caring for all of God's people and courageousness through living a Christ-centered life. She brought me to meet other Baptist leaders at Ordination Council gatherings. In order to complete the ordination process, I needed to compose a long paper on my theological understandings, my spiritual journey, and the role of the church in the world. Rev. Marnette Saz helped prepare me for my Ordination Council. She said to remember Soul Freedom as an important Baptist principle. I believed Soul Freedom to be comparable to the Roman Catholic principle of conscience, which I had steeped myself in. While we study the teachings of our faith, the Bible, and our traditions, in the final analysis it is our conscience, our soul freedom between our soul and God's direction, that determines our call and our most important decisions.

My theological paper declared:

As an artist my work was once praised for its "flukiness." Now I praise God for the flukiness of calling me to the Baptist way of faithfulness. The concreteness of Jesus, the prophetic tradition, the emotional hymns are sympathetic, or what is called in Italian *simpatico*. It is a faith where I don't have to cut off my feelings from my mind. And it is a faith that has remained strong in the face of oppression; it has nurtured the great Civil Rights Movement. I want to be a part of a local church and a faith with guts.

The call to a ministry of healing is a call given to those who have known brokenness in our own lives yet are willing to be present to others' griefs and struggles. It became even more clear that healing ministry was the natural outgrowth of my desire to counsel, to reach out as a pastor to the grieving and oppressed, and to bring the joy of art and music to the dry and lifeless places. The desire was big and my heart held an expansive optimism.

The time preceding my ordination was a sad one in the life of Old Cambridge Baptist Church. A conflict simmering between the pastor, Monica, and the parish administrator came to a head within our congregation. The long efforts of late night congregational meetings and hours of facilitators failed, and the church was at an impasse. Late in the evening on the Friday before my Ordination Council, which was scheduled for Sunday afternoon, a decision was reached. While not unanimous, the congregation voted that both staff resign their positions. I felt devastated. As a lesbian, I wanted to hang on to the robe of the woman whom I had followed into the risks of ordained ministry. Moreover, a few weeks earlier I had swallowed my pride and begged Monica to reschedule a personal family commitment in order to attend my Ordination Council. "I need you to be there." It now became her last official duty. How hard it must have been for her to be there.

My Council was a success, but my pastor, Monica, who inspired my call to ordination, was gone. I was left grieving and wondering about the brokenness of the church and the difficulties facing women and gay pastors, foreshadowing events that were to unfold in my own ministry. I was asked to give the first sermon after she left. I spoke about Aaron receiving the charge to carry on the work of Moses. Moses led his people but could not himself enter the promised land. It so impressed the congregation that an impromptu meeting occurred after church to consider me to become the interim pastor. It was not to be. I wondered if I was destined to spark, inspire, move others from the side lines. This was not the first time. At times I became frustrated to not be given more opportunities to shine brighter and provide leadership. My Baptist colleague told me on the phone that as a woman in ministry, "you need to learn to blow your own horn." Are horns the only part of the orchestra?

June 11, 1989, Old Cambridge Baptist Church

Ordination

The Fourth Call: 1988–90

That day in June coalesced my passion for life, community, and justice, culminating in a grand celebration of an eight year faith journey.

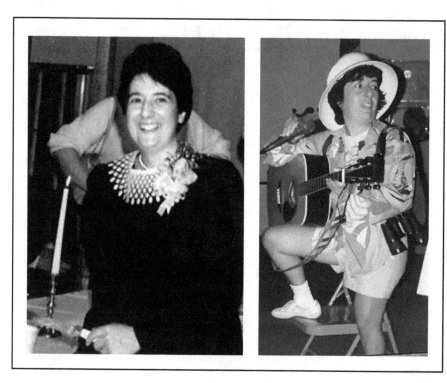

[left] Installation as Associate Pastor [right] Vacation Bible School

TWENTY-NINE

Leaving Boston for New England

THE CALL CAME ONE EVENING WHEN JUDY'S PARENTS WERE VISITING FROM Cleveland.

"Would you like to interview for a part-time associate pastor position?" Would I ever, I thought.

The next week I left my Boston neighborhood and drove south to a quiet country setting, colored a brilliant dark red by the cranberry bogs in the fall, I was buoyed by hopes and fears of what might lie ahead.

A small committee interviewed me and invited me to become their first female associate pastor. The white wooden New England church stood at the center of town, originally the First Baptist Church before the merging of two other parishes. Three denominations maintained ecclesial identity while agreeing to unite as one parish. I would be visiting elderly members and new members, supporting the Christian education program, and preaching once a month.

Ned, the senior pastor, and I divided our time between the three denominations for their regional clergy meetings; he covered the Methodist, I covered the Baptist, and we split the functions of the United Church of Christ. As new members expressed interest in joining the church, I drove out to their homes to meet their spouses, children, and pets to talk about what mattered to them. Older folk tended to have strong denominational ties from the past and could easily choose which denomination to affiliate with. I gave a short explanation of each denomination for the people who didn't know which one to join. One key difference in practice was communion, served once a month. In the Methodist tradition the people came forward to the altar like in my Catholic past, but the other two denominations received the elements in their pews. Cranberry juice was served instead of grape.

Ned grew up in the town. His pastorate spanned most of his ministry. A big man with broad shoulders, round red face, and thick dark brown hair, he seemed uncomfortable, almost embarrassed, to be working with a female pastor as he drove me around in his pick-up truck to show me the town. We stopped and had coffee at a local place filled with hunched-over men with caps who had known him for years.

I tried to carve out a niche for myself. The entry of women into the ministry was often fraught with issues as the senior pastor was almost always a man, usually with no experience in working professionally with a woman. The religious bodies didn't do a lot to help us find ways to work together. The all-male clergy groups at that time didn't shepherd us along either.

In spite of our odd-couple leadership relationship, the first year went well. Looking back on it, the setting had similarities to my VISTA town in Kansas. I drove everywhere, still confused by NSEW directions, and visited people in their homes. I was loved and appreciated by elderly and new members whose lives were less busy and had more space to share.

On Sunday mornings, the parish hall filled with a hundred children from ages five to fifteen. I led worship and played guitar before they went off to their classes. A favorite song to the tune of "Louie, Louie" we all moved to "Egyptian-style" was "Pharaoh, Pharaoh, Oh baby let my people go!"

During the next hour I assisted Ned at the second service. One Sunday a month I preached at both services, affording me the chance to preach twice and grow in confidence. The choir director was a gifted jazz pianist. I joined the choir with Ned and Pastor Bill, the retired pastor who had held my position. What fun!

As I prepared to be formally installed in the position six months after I arrived, I was interviewed for the paper in Plymouth by a veteran journalist. She raved about Rev. Dr. Peter Gomes, African American minister at Harvard Memorial Church, a local Baptist boy from Plymouth who had made good. Years later I heard Dr. Gomes speak at a pastor's conference. A former Republican with a sophisticated bearing and way of speaking, he came out as a gay man and became a prophetic figure for us. I imagined in some way I might walk in his footsteps though my Bostonian speech did not rise to the level of his erudite Harvard inflection.

One day I was asked to officiate at a funeral of a woman as Ned was on vacation. She had lived next door to the former Methodist Church. An old timer, Gertrude was part of the large Finnish community that worked on the cranberry bogs. A tall ladder leaned against the old wooden church. Her family was giving the church a fresh coat of paint to prepare for the funeral. I shook hands with Gertrude's grieving husband, and we strolled through her gardens as he spoke about his love for his wife.

My heart opened wide as I heard the hymn "Finlandia" sung in this miniature church. My ears and eyes breathed in its beauty as I grew to appreciate the miracle of nature, cherished faith, and quiet bonds of this tight community. After the service, the crowd of neighbors and family left the church and gathered next door at her home to share a common meal under a tent. My eulogy celebrated Gertrude, the gardener and mother, and spoke of the earth she cared for that now was caring for her:

On Wednesday I will commit her to the earth.
She who tended her garden, whose testimony is the Sunflower, the Formosa tree, the Clematis.
Gertrude, sister, I bid you join the Heavenly array that makes the earth full of splendor and not a desert of dust.
On Wednesday I will commit her to the earth.
She, who tended her garden, returns.

I was formally installed in my position that fall. Though it poured all day with strong winds, my mother and brother Anthony, and my aunts and uncles all managed to get there from Boston. Auntie Rosie and Uncle Connie, my godparents Anna and Dom, Auntie Portia, my mother's sisters Lena and Rose, my great aunt Josie and cousins Rose and Dom. I wore a dark blue velvet dress with a lace collar that Johnny had bought me. I looked like a proper New England church pastor. I had left ethnic Boston to become a Yankee New Englander!

Deacon Marty Hackett from Old Cambridge Baptist Church gave the charge to me: "I charge you to remember that this is only one branch of God's family. There are many other branches, people from all walks of life and many religious persuasions with whom you can work for social justice and peace. God has blessed us with a large family. I call on you to use your powers of discernment to recognize God and God's power and help from whatever source they may come."

These words were to foreshadow the days and years ahead when I would need to make tough decisions as I experienced pain and betrayal in ministry.

THIRTY

Italian Protestant

Your ordination bears dramatic witness to a
creative, dynamic, and incarnational God.

— Deacon Pat Guerrini, prayer given at the author's ordination

MY BROTHER ANTHONY FILLED THE LARGE GOTHIC CHURCH WITH CYPRESS trees and red geraniums. He christened it "Italian Protestant." Our sexton, a refugee and university teacher from El Salvador, labored for weeks bringing new life into the sanctuary, climbing up the Corinthian columns to add a fresh coat of paint. My stepfather, now in his eighties, in and out of the hospital, grieved that he was too frail to come and handed me a couple of hundred dollar bills to buy a robe for my ordination, an off-white simple garment of Belgian linen from the Catholic liturgical store. Having completed a year in my pastorate, it was time for the ordination ceremony. I was filled with anticipation, playing "One Moment in Time" by Whitney Houston over and over again in my car tape player as I flew down Memorial Drive.

The weather was perfect on June 11, 1989 at Old Cambridge Baptist Church. A video taken outside showed a short, stocky woman in a red cotton dress ambling up the granite steps toward the bright red door of the gray stone church. It was Heidi! A yellow school bus pulled into the driveway. Ned, red-faced from the heat and stress of getting to the church on time, monitored his flock into the sanctuary. Ralph, a Baptist pastor who reminded me of the all-embracing nature of Jupiter, opened the service with an old-fashioned Baptist hymn sing.

The immensity of life, given and embraced through the many paths I had crossed, became apparent to me as I turned my head and looked across the sanctuary. Amazingly, the church was filled. I saw people who would never have found themselves together: Italian Catholics from the Verro-chi and Ierardi sides of the family, neighbors, girlfriends I had grown up with, Healthsigns friends, seminary friends from Andover-Newton and Episcopal Divinity School, American Baptists, Congregationalists, and Methodists from my present ministry. A technicolor parade of my life so far. I was overwhelmed with joy.

Anthony, the last to sit down after putting the finishing touches on the flowers, cracked the pew, causing giggles to ripple through the rows where my family sat. One of the deacons rushed over in a panic. Cousin Dominic declared, "These pews can't hold Italians."

My parish broke into a spirited jazz interpretation of Amazing Grace. The OCBC choir sang Gounod's Sanctus; Mary, our choir soprano sounded like an angel.

I was honored that my seminary professor Rev. Dr. Katie Cannon consented to preach. My cousin Les read the scripture she chose from 2 Samuel: "If only I could have a drink of water from home!" David is in the middle of battle, in the middle of what he knew to be a danger-ous life-threatening situation. He was lonely and filled with longing for something familiar, something that makes you feel taken care of. Dr. Cannon knew from her own experiences and inner wisdom that there would be times in my ministry when I, too, would long for that drink of water from home.

Rev. Betsy Sowers supported me in naming my commitments to God and the community.

Rev. Dr. Jay Warden presented me with the Certificate of Ordination:

I hope that you will tell the story of the day that you were ordained kneeling in front of the communion table of Old Cambridge Baptist Church, the communion table that stretches around the world, because a man from Burma was here today (President of the Baptists of Burma), it also stretches historically back into the ages of time as people gathered around the table to celebrate the family and worship and as you are moving into the future many people are going to want to come and sit at your table and eat and fellowship and find sustenance of life.

Rev. Dr. Meg Hess invited everyone to join in the laying on of hands: clergy, family, and friends. I knelt and felt this enormous loving presence pressing on my head and shoulders. After Meg's moving prayer, I was relieved to be helped to my feet by my seminary pal Rev. Sylvia Robinson.

A gorgeous quilted stole symbolic of water and light, designed by Sue Turbak, was presented to me by deacons Leslie and Bill of OCBC.

Healthsigns presented me with a stained-glass flower and our logo: "You have been called by God to a ministry of wholeness, mutuality, empowered by God's love through community." Judy said, "Healthsigns has been a place as well as an idea for us, and we have worked and lived toward a clearer understanding of what life to the full can be."

Rev. Barbara Smith-Moran crafted me an emerald-colored silk stole brought back by her husband, Jim, who had recently returned from China during the Tiananmen Square uprising.

My cousin Pat Guerrini, a Roman Catholic deacon, offered his blessing: "Through ordination you have been granted a special opportunity to touch and transform the lives of your sisters and brothers with that strength, grace, and sensitivity bestowed on you as a holy woman of God . . . If we would only allow ourselves then to experience that true passion we feel today . . . we can transform the world with that burning desire to love God."

Rev. Jay Warden's prediction came to pass as many people did come to my table to eat and find sustenance of life. And in trying times, I remembered the story of my family and friends who gathered that day to share with me God's richest blessings.

THIRTY-ONE

Telling the Truth in Love

We may no longer be children, tossed to and fro by the waves and carried about by every wind of doctrine, by human cunning, by craftiness in deceitful schemes. Rather, speaking the truth in love, we are to grow up in every way into him who is the head, into Christ.

—Ephesians 4:14–15 (ESV)

THE SECOND YEAR IN MY PARISH FELT HEAVY. IN ORDER TO LIVE CLOSER TO southeastern Massachusetts, Judy and I moved to Cape Cod, but I missed my life in Boston. In the church newsletter I wrote:

> I am looking forward to my first autumn on Cape Cod. I love walking on the beach in the early evening, the sense of serenity and openness I feel in God's presence. Since I moved here this summer with my friend Judy, we feel grateful that God has led us to such a beautiful place. Judy began a position as a rehabilitation physician in Hyannis and works with people who are brain injured, many of them in comas. It's strange how there can be so much suffering in the midst of beauty.

While my outer self was engaged and busy serving my congregation, my personal self could not come out and be shared fully without risking my job. I needed this church position to fulfill the odd requirement to complete three years of parish ministry before being certified as a pastoral counselor.

Unbeknownst to me, a small group of people were plotting ways to terminate my job. I thought it might be related to the Christian Education committee led by some fundamentalist women. Whatever it was or wasn't, they masked their plans by not creating a democratic process, thereby working outside the rest of the congregation.

After the Herculean effort of completing my doctorate degree, totally unacknowledged by the church, I sensed I might become more of a threat to Ned. I sensed I would need to leave there in the near future, but thought I could do so at the right time. I had much to be proud of: my creative approaches with the children, my ability to listen to the elders with compassion, and my work to empower more women in the community. I initiated a woman's retreat that we held at the Craigville Conference Center on the Cape for two consecutive years. We met at Seaside House in the fall, soaking up the splendid views overlooking the marshes and wildlife. Twelve women, including the pastor's wife and the church secretary, had a chance to relax and tend to their own spiritual and communal needs as we enjoyed good food, song, and laughter, celebrating the goodness of nature and God.

The week after the retreat was Laity Sunday when lay people are invited to participate in the service. In the past, mainly individuals who were already comfortable speaking publicly in church were given a role. My idea was to get all the retreat women to participate. At first try they held back, not wanting to be at the lectern, not feeling they had something important to say. Though I was disappointed, I could identify with their fear. Finally, I left them alone to work it out themselves, advising them to trust in the action of the Holy Spirit. Ned sidled up to me and said in his usual matter-of-fact apologetic tone: "You won't get them to be up there; maybe one or two."

Sunday came and, one by one, seven women shared their reflections about the retreat and its influence on their spiritual lives. The Holy Spirit triumphed in flying colors that day. In my monthly letter to the parish I wrote of my gratitude:

> It is through our gifts that we glorify God. Through our uniqueness we give thanks to God for having made us. As the Psalmist says, "Lift up your heads, O gates! And be lifted up, O ancient doors! That the king of glory may come in." It is hard for most of us to put ourselves forward. We feel self-conscious or anxious. I recall being in speech class in the 7th grade. I had to give a talk. I got up in front of the class, quickly said what I had to and sat down. The teacher said, "Anne, now do that again, this time don't look at the ceiling." Never did I imagine I'd be preaching twenty years later and that one day, my seventh grade teacher, Frank Fornaro, would come to church and hear me as he himself was in the process of becoming a priest after years of teaching. When God calls we can express our gratitude and open the closed doors in our lives to give God the glory.

The announcement that my position was terminated was hard for me. "There is a price to pay for silence, but there is often a worse price to pay for words of truth." I felt blindsided, not to mention humiliated, bewildered, and angry. I decided I would not do what was easiest: disappear. That coming Sunday was my turn to preach as Ned would be on his hunting expedition. I would find a way to convey the truth of what happened to me the previous Sunday. The appointed lectionary scripture for that Sunday—"telling the truth in love"—was perfect!

Sunday morning I held myself tight as I sat on the red velvet cushioned "throne" behind the altar. A kind elder in the parish, Mr. Wells, did the opening prayers and scripture readings. It was not unusual when I preached to receive the full attention of the congregation; often one could even "hear a pin drop." I wondered which people in the congregation were aware of the news that I was fired. I rose up to preach, and as I was standing in the pulpit, I was surprised to see Ned sitting alone in the balcony; he had come home a day early from his hunting trip! No turning back now.

I took a breath and began: "Last Sunday after church when the Pastoral Relations Committee told me they were not going to renew my contract due to economic factors, I was stunned."

Phoebe, one of the older members seated in the middle of the church, emotionally fragile and dependent on me for my regular visits to her trailer home, let out a gasp at the news. I knew from the turmoil in the pews how little the congregation knew. I continued:

> There was no room for discussion or sharing of feelings. I was most upset because of how it was presented and done by one committee without including me or coming up with a mutual plan for termination. I was hurt that Pastor Ned didn't speak with me as a colleague, as a human being, and as the senior pastor of this church.

> I learned from my father's death that truth should be told. So today I want to tell the truth in love in the presence of God and the congregation who called me just over two years ago. I believe there is no greater truth than God's call to love one another, to find ways to speak and reach out to each other, imagining the wild possibility that we might love someone as much as we love ourselves. The profound truth we heard in this morning's gospel is none other than a word waiting to be spoken. Who will speak the word of the Lord? What Jesus believes we need in the world is not a new way of thinking nor a new political agenda but a revolutionary new way of being together as human beings . . . we can't know about love until we can love somebody so much that whatever hurt is done to them, it is done to us.

Ned did not talk to me for over a week, though the parish secretary winked at me. Ned's cousin came in the next day and lectured him sternly, and then she came over to me, tearful but strong. "I am sorry for what happened. It was wrong. Someday you will be older and develop tougher skin." The retired Baptist organist also railed against the church and assured me that "This will never happen again here because the church will follow a congregational system and install its clergy properly by vote of the congregation."

My time at the church would be over at Christmas so I had about six weeks to go. What might have been a horrible and tense waiting period turned out for me to be some of my best days there. I reached out, in spite of my vulnerability, visiting not only the new members and elders but the church leaders, younger families, anyone who wished to see me. I especially was touched by a girl in our Sunday School. Her mother went into the kitchen and opened the cabinet to show me the little plastic communion cup her daughter had saved from the Sunday I had visited each class of the younger children, teaching them how special it is to receive communion. The kids and I reverently shared the bread and the cups of cranberry juice.

I preached for the last time in the first week of December. My parting words were:

> What I'll most treasure is our talks together, discussing topics that are easy as well as difficult. I'll remember the stories you've shared with me, the questions you had about what it meant to be a Christian, a man, a woman, a parent, not to mention a Baptist, a Methodist, a Congregationalist. We've had many of those conversations too. Some of you have shared your hopes of the future with me. Others have looked back and shown me pictures of your past. You've shown me what you value in life. "Where your treasure is there will your heart be." Three Sundays ago I told you how my position was terminated and some of my feelings about it. Since then, seeds of communication and sharing have been planted. My mother told me recently that she and her two sisters had been praying that I find a position closer to home so I don't have to drive on those dark roads in bad weather. My wise-cracking brother called me from California when he heard the news about my leaving. He said: "See what prayer will do!"

THIRTY-TWO

Living the Gospel

*Why Luke? Because he more than the others humanized this
man, this prophet, Jesus, for us. He speaks of parties and
celebrations. Jesus has a good time and always with the poor.*

— Kip Tiernan

NEW BEDFORD WAS A CITY THAT I HAD VISITED ONCE WHEN JOHNNY brought me to see their Whaling Museum. Over the years I read stories in the Boston papers about crime and poverty there. Traveling from Cape Cod to New Bedford on Interstate 195, I beheld a city emerging past the forests of southeast Massachusetts. After getting off the quiet highway brightened by the Atlantic coast, I drove through the downtown streets dark with shadows of buildings before climbing up the hill to County Street to the pastoral counseling center. The Interfaith Center was in a historical stone building that was originally a stately home with rich woodwork and tiled fireplaces; such homes were popular during the turn of the twentieth century.

At this training center of the American Association of Pastoral Counselors, I would be able to work toward the experience and credentialing I needed. New Bedford was a poor city but only in terms of economics. Our center's outreach brought astonishing people to us of all backgrounds, races, and ethnicities from the city and neighboring towns. I left home at nine in the morning on Mondays and departed the center around eight in the evening. Three hours of individual and group supervision sandwiched in between meeting with counselees. Our staff included Baptist, Congregational, and Unitarian ministers; Catholic Sisters; a hospital and a campus chaplain. All were certified pastoral counselors and psychologists. We saw over one hundred people a week for whatever they could pay in cash or through insurance. No one was ever turned away.

Many of the people I counseled remain vivid in my mind. The warm-hearted Portuguese seamstress abandoned by her gambling and drinking husband, her drawn-out divorce, her helpless and pleading voice commingled with her strength and courage to attend Al-Anon meetings. She voiced her dilemma, common among ethnic women, of having to reconcile loyalty to her dysfunctional family with her desire for self-respect and autonomy.

And dear Grace, so weak, small, emaciated, shaking with anxiety; how lucky we were to meet that first day as it was a rare occasion that I was asked to do an intake. "My son is a counselor. He and my doctor said if I didn't come for help I would soon be dead. Can I stay with you as my counselor? I feel safe in your calm presence." Fifty years of marriage gone in a heartbeat; her devoted spouse killed on his prized motorcycle. The parish priest forgot to visit her after the funeral. As she told me her life story, the truth of her unresolved grief became apparent; she was carrying guilt from her father's death thirty years previously. One year later she wrote to me and to the director of my program. She said she was smiling and volunteering at a Catholic elementary school near her home. She wore the button I gave her to remind her to stop calling herself stupid. The button was from my friend, the wonderful Dr. Ruth Harriet Jacobs, a specialist in the joys of aging. It read: RASP: Remarkably Aging Smart Person.

I experienced pleasure and internal changes working with my counselees. Although supported, I was also challenged by my relationships with staff. In our large interdisciplinary group with six senior staff and seven of us in training, I kept mum unless I had to present a case for discussion. The senior psychologist called me Calvin, after our speechless

thirtieth president. Once someone gave a presentation on a client grieving a loss. A senior staff person commented that it was time to "get over
it." I said my father's been gone twenty-five years, and I haven't "gotten
over it." Sister Madeline, a cocky, smart Dominican nun, responded to
my feelings about not getting as far as I had wanted with a Greek-American woman whose case I presented one afternoon: "She came in for a
touch-up job and you wanted to paint the whole house."

I feared I wasn't good enough to be accepted by the senior staff,
though I didn't know how I would know when good enough was reached.
But I believed I was good enough because I got results and could sense
clients' love and respect for me.

Rev. Dr. John Waters was my second supervisor. John had thick,
dark, slicked-back hair and wore a brown leather jacket. I even think he
swaggered, though maybe I imagined it. Forceful and direct, he called
me "young lady" once too often.

"I am not a young lady," I said quietly but firmly.

"What do you want me to call you?" he asked in his gruff voice.

"Anne is fine."

One day he took a blunt tack with me about a counseling situation. I
surprised him by saying I wasn't going to talk about my client if he continued in that vein. He responded, "It's all grist for the mill." He leaned
back in a chair and said in a pensive way: "Yes, it is an unusual, lonely
calling. You see the depth of people's pain and then you leave here and go
out into a superficial world."

Funny how eventually we took to each other; I gleaned a lot from
him. Years later I ran into him at a professional conference; he told me he
loved me and gave me a big embrace. Maybe that's when you know you
are good enough.

Ways of loving—that was the key to my work in New Bedford. Life
was more "in the raw" there, like at St. Luke's Parish and Worcester State
Hospital, and Hospice a few years later. Many shades of people touched
my life like a colorful palette of possibilities about to flower on an open
canvas, what Dr. Martin Luther King, Jr. called the beloved community.

Pierre was a tall handsome Cape Verdean man trying to cultivate his
own goodness and kick his addiction so he could love his own child. He
told me about an epiphany he had with his priest as a young man on retreat. The priest had told Pierre that he was able to love because Jesus had
first loved him. As a wise spiritual director had told me, "The Catholic
Church taught us to love God, then our neighbor, then ourselves, but we
can't love God or neighbor until we learn to love ourselves first." Pierre
no longer lived with the mother of his little girl, but he would visit his
"opportunity child," praying that she would know love too.

Sometimes my pastoral counseling sessions were quite brief yet dramatic. Adelia feared her husband, who had rifles hanging on their walls. She too was tough with a strong patina of anger covering her hurt. Intuitively, I invited her to do a guided relaxation; her throat became unblocked and the hurt and tears flowed out. We worked out a plan for dealing with the husband and she grew stronger and kinder toward herself. Adelia swore like a trooper during sessions. When she realized during our last session that I was "a priest," she was mortified, apologizing profusely for her language as we walked together outside in the sun. I smiled and said it was OK.

Undoubtedly, the saddest and most horrific encounter I had at Interfaith was with a twelve-year-old boy. In "old country" ethnic families, mothers were accustomed to discipline by force. Marco was dragged into my office late one afternoon by my client, his mother, for not behaving. Marco looked so lost, his deep brown eyes hidden, showing confusion and desperation, yet wanting to grow up like the other boys. While walking home from school one day, he was attacked by an older kid. Worse than this attack, he had seen his father bruise his mother's tongue with a knife. Witnessing that trauma led him to stop talking, metaphorically losing his own tongue. While his speech was slowly returning, I knew conversation would not be an effective mode of counseling. My words were saved for his mother who was on the brink of forfeiting her home because of her gambling macho husband whom she was afraid to confront. My caring for Marco energized my firm directive to his mother to get financial advice, which I helped her acquire, and to stand up to her husband for the love of her two boys. As for Marco, we played chess in the director's office, a game he learned in school but had no one at home to play with. I talked a little; he talked even less, but my strategy worked and life improved at home.

In contrast, my strategy with Ron, the director of the center, was less effective. I wanted to increase my hours at the center as I loved working there and needed to make a decent income after losing my position at the parish. Ron was an amiable man who was good at matching clients with me and often let me use his beautiful and spacious office with a tiled fireplace. Ron assured me I could receive insurance reimbursement through my supervisor's license, carefully going over the figures with me. What he didn't tell me was that the supervisor's license had lapsed. I don't know for sure that Ron knew this, but later when it came out, I was incensed as he continued to make promises he couldn't keep all the while smiling and encouraging me. Without insurance I averaged fifteen dollars a session as most clients had little money to spare. I had one intense blow-up in his office, then I realized it was no use. He acted helpless. But he still held all the power.

After two years, I left the center, receiving their permission to invite a few clients to continue to see me on the Cape. My time in New Bedford, gentle on my mind, remains some of the best of my ministry due to my clients, my colleagues, and my growing confidence as a pastoral therapist. Unfortunately, the center continued to lose income sources because of changing insurance regulations and limitations on pastoral counseling in Massachusetts. No longer was the center able to offer high quality counseling to over 100 people a week. In retrospect I was witnessing the early days of the forced diminishment of my profession, which eventually resulted in an increasing lack of emotional and spiritual health that spread like a virus across our cities. What would lie ahead for me as I focused my energy on life and work on Cape Cod?

Provincetown

Sicily

Spain and Portugal

Jazz Ladies: Billie Holiday, Ella Fitzgerald, Anita O'Day, Carmen McRae

Jazz Ladies: Lena Horne, Alberta Hunter,
Dinah Washington, Nina Simone

At Home on Cape Cod

Bass Hole Abstract

Appreciation

Poppy Showings

That's Amore

Mystic Sunset

Rolling Water

Cape Cod Landscapes 2021

Libra Studio I

Fall

Cape Cod Artist

The Fifth Call: 1990–2005

I shared my passion for art with Marion on my pastoral visits to her at the convalescent home. Looking closely at prints of my work, she declared: "I know the ministry is a noble profession, but don't neglect your art."

[top] Duchy paintings [bottom] Thanksgiving with family

THIRTY-THREE

On Cape Cod

There is so much beauty in being open to our God-given selves.
Sexual openness and openness to God are two very sacred and
fragile dimensions of life. Pastoral counselors can offer both a
sanctuary and a sacred wisdom to make the wounded whole.

—Anne Ierardi, in *Dialogue*, published by American Baptist Churches, USA

THE CAPE HAS A QUIET BEAUTY, BUT IT IS FAR DIFFERENT FROM THE RICHES I had known in Boston. What, I wondered, might lie ahead? Here I found myself minus positions in a church or a counseling center. Still, I had been ordained, completed my doctorate, and pastoral counseling certificates hung on the wall. A wonderful opportunity emerged through the American Baptist Churches to design and edit a journal issue for pastoral counselors and chaplains throughout the United States. It featured an article I wrote on women and faith development, the topic of my doctoral project. But it was only for two issues.

Slowly my work at Healthsigns expanded with clients plus a group healing from sexual abuse. I remodeled our attached garage into a waiting room and bravely hung up my new paintings. Judy had a demanding job as the doctor in a center that treated people who had suffered brain and spinal cord injuries, many of whom were young people who had been in accidents. She put a lot of effort into working with grieving and often angry families trying to deal with these tragedies.

The help I needed came when Rev. Ellen Chahey, Director of the Council of Churches, informed me of an interim associate position at a church in Orleans. I interviewed. I was astonished and excited when one of the elder female deacons asked me if I had a commitment to social justice ministry. Another deacon took me on a tour of the church, confiding in me how caring the congregation had been to her after her husband had died. When I got the call to come work with Pastor Kim Cartwright, I gladly accepted the part-time position at the Federated Church of Orleans.

Since there were so many elders in the church, there was always a lot of visiting to do. Pam, our parish administrator, radiated an energetic caring presence and would clue me into the immediate needs of the people needing support. I would then make a mental note: Mary had a stroke and is paralyzed. I will visit her at the hospital after my ultrasound to see how the cyst on my left ovary is faring. And while I am there I will look in on Russ, the old full-bearded lobster fisherman and native Cape Codder who wouldn't set foot in the church on Sundays, but I think he liked my visit last year when he had a hip replacement. Kim mentioned to me that Phoebe was feeling guilty and thought God was punishing her. Phoebe, tall and erect, was raised in a strict Dutch Reformed Church. She and I had deepened our connection after I had visited her in her stately colonial home when suddenly her phone rang with the news that her favorite nephew had died of AIDS. While she couldn't help but be judgmental toward her nephew's gay friends, she did call to mind her own experience when she was ready to marry and had to go against the wishes of her church and minister. Eventually, she sold her home and moved into a beautiful apartment in an assisted-living facility. Several months later, she had a stroke. Her doctor planned to send her two hours away off the Cape for rehabilitation. I was quite familiar with the rehab facilities on the Cape since Judy worked in several, so I went to his office on a Friday afternoon to request that he keep Phoebe nearby so friends and church members could visit her. The doctor came out of his office. He was a big man, with strong features, and walked with a cane. He glared at me and said, "Who is going to visit her? You? Are you getting a commission for this?" I left disgusted. That Monday the news came that the doctor had suddenly died of a heart attack.

Fall was approaching. The best of times and the worst of times were about to descend on my life like a train wreck, in astrological language "a Uranus cycle." The senior pastor requested a sabbatical less than eight months after I arrived; I welcomed the opportunity to have more responsibilities, but I also knew it would bring more stress. I was fortunate to have two retired male clergy as assistants whom I grew to love and rely on.

In the meantime, the continuing need to include, welcome, and acknowledge gay persons in congregations faced fierce opposition. Healthsigns Center joined several churches across the country as a founding member of a group we called Welcome and Affirming Baptists (AWAB). As more and more clergy were coming out of the closet and churches were beginning to address homophobia in their congregations, we needed to band together. As our numbers grew, the Massachusetts Baptist Conference issued a statement of support while the national denomination wrestled with conservative churches, particularly in Ohio, parts of California, and West Virginia. These churches began seceding from their associations. One of the California associations would not allow any AWAB congregations to belong. This disaster they termed "disfellowship."

My friend Rev. Mark Crosby took a bold step and came out nationally as a gay pastoral counselor. Conservatives voted to freeze his endorsement from the National Office of Pastoral Counselors and Chaplains. Mark and I had coauthored an article on sexuality and spirituality for the second American Baptist journal I had edited. I received an email notice to be careful about what was in my file at National Ministries, as I could potentially lose my endorsement as a pastoral counselor from the denomination headquarters!

In late October I was due to present myself for an oral review for the next level: Fellow membership in the American Association of Pastoral Counselors. Now that my standing as a pastoral counselor was threatened, and since I felt a good fit in the United Church of Christ (UCC) through the local churches I had served, it made perfect sense for me to change denominations. I spoke to a colleague and friend in the UCC to request an interview with his committee to transfer my denominational standing from American Baptist to UCC.

However, an odd thing occurred at the Hyannis hospital the day I was visiting my parishioners. Brent, the hospital chaplain and chair of the UCC committee, took me aside in the hospital's tiny chapel.

"I don't think it is a good idea for you to apply for standing in the UCC."

Shocked, I replied, "How can the committee advise me before I've submitted any paperwork?" I felt betrayed by this man with whom I had come to share a common interest in healing over the past five years. How could they get away with not following their own procedures as published in their manual on the ministry?

Since this made no logical sense to me and still not willing to believe that politics and discrimination could so easily become bed partners, I went ahead, submitted my documents to the committee, and appeared for the interview. I sensed tension in the room, and the questioning was more confrontational than collegial. My trust level with the committee was low as I had heard rumors of gender and sexual orientation bias, so it was impossible for me to share the threat that hung over me from the American Baptist rising tide of anti-gay actions. In a real sense, I was seeking asylum in the UCC, but instead I came face to face with the very issues I was fleeing from. A week later I received a letter in the mail saying they had voted unanimously against my request. (Years later I learned this to be false as one of my female colleagues told me she had voted in my favor.)

Discouraged by the outcome of the association, I also was under stress from a counseling field education seminar I was leading. At the outset, the students arrived unhappy with their field assignments. I was unable to bond with many of them, and they took their frustrations out on me.

In mid-October I woke up in pain in the middle of the night. "Something wasn't right," as in my favorite childhood story, "Madeline," when "Miss Clavel turned on the light." I felt funny but attributed it to my emotional pain from the rejection and the stress in nearing my oral pastoral counselors review. At 3 a.m. I put on the video of my ordination and listened to Katie Cannon's sermon about the challenges of ministry. In that moment her words made more sense to me than when she had given the sermon.

The next morning, Sunday, I led a worship service in a nursing home. Since the home was across the street from the Cape Cod Hospital, I decided to visit six patients from my church. That afternoon, I attended a work party with Judy. I still wasn't feeling right. When we got home I took a strong laxative, assuming it would take care of my problem.

Monday afternoon I called Judy's beeper. I was in so much pain I could hardly walk. Judy said she would come right home as we needed to go to the emergency room. "There's a doctor I know who can help you."

Dr. Brooks, a gentle, youthful-looking man, responded quickly with a series of tests. As I lay on the table scared and bloated with liquid, in more pain as the ultrasound wand did circles around my stomach, I listened to the radiologist's comments. "I see gallstones, urinary infection, ovarian cyst, and clouds around the appendix." Dr. Brooks put his hand on me and said, "I think the pressing problem is the appendix, but we can't tell for sure. I want to operate now."

Given my imagination, the idea of someone cutting into my abdomen was terrifying. Dr. Brooks looked kindly into my eyes and said, "If you were my mother or sister, I would do this."

How could I know he was telling the truth? I had met enough two-faced professional males in my career already.

"Can I go home and think about it?" I asked.

Dr. Brooks said patiently, "You can stay here overnight and think about it."

They brought me upstairs to a semi-private room. The damn laxative began to work overtime! Then came the fever. All night I was back and forth with my IV to the bathroom. My roommate, an older German lady, was a great comfort; I wish I could have met her again to thank her. In her thick accent she assured me: "Don't worry. You learn to roll with the punches. The man upstairs is watching out for you." Early next morning Dr. Brooks appeared with a clipboard. I quickly signed permission papers, saw Judy for a moment, and was wheeled off to surgery.

Dr. Brooks saved my life that morning; I had a ruptured appendix with peritonitis. I didn't even know what it meant until afterward. Nothing else they found, gallstones and an ovarian cyst, could be safely removed at that time. They left the wound open for dressings for five days. The only bed available in the hospital was on the pediatric ward. My roommate was a borderline addict who blasted the television and made dramatic scenes in bed with her boyfriend. I was on a morphine pump. My body was a mess, but my mind was vigilant and my dreams wild. Nights were difficult, so I just pumped away until a night nurse scolded me for overdoing it. I thought they had said I should use it as needed. I was anxious to get out of bed. As I walked past the nurse's station, they commented on my "marathon." One day I snuck over to the next ward with my IV and visited one of the ladies from my church whom I had been concerned about. I don't think she ever forgot that visit from her wounded healer.

Thankfully, they gave me a cute private room after a few days. It had a border of little fishes swimming on the blue and yellow wallpaper. The sexual healing group I facilitated sent a nurse from the group to visit. She walked in and declared, "I know you appreciate the inner child, but this is going too far!"

I loved my stay in the little private room until the day an intern stitched me up without enough anesthesia. The nurse understood my cries but the young man just kept doing his job. I understand now that drugs work slowly in my body. Maybe I should not have been so nice and said no to interns. Every morning at 5 a.m. I was stunned by the fluorescent light turned on by an Asian intern who gently patted my stomach. "Distended?" she politely asked, as if she didn't know. Instead of being angry, I almost bowed, if I could have made it out of bed.

Brent, the chaplain, never appeared during the week I was there. After he and his committee had rejected my request for denominational standing in the UCC, Brent approached me one day as I was preparing to visit some parishioners at the hospital.

Sidling up to me, he said, "I am really so sorry about what happened at the meeting last week." I replied, "If you are so sorry, why did you do it?" and I stomped out of the room.

The day after surgery my mother had her oldest sister, Rose, drive "the three sisters," Rose, Lena, and Theresa, to the hospital from Boston. I did my best to look alive. My mother, also sensitive to hospitals and sickness, always visited me the day after surgery to reassure herself. She surprised me with a Madeline doll.

Before I knew how to read, I identified with my heroine Madeline in Paris.

"Read this book to me, MaMa!" I cried. MaMa, my father's mother, paused, then began to tell me a different story, perhaps one of the folk tales from Italy she learned as a child.

"No, MaMa. That's not how it goes!" I exclaimed, not realizing that MaMa couldn't read English.

Like me, Madeline was the smallest in her group. She had spunk and was very brave. When she confronted the orange-striped tiger in the zoo, I shouted along with my pal in Paris, "Pooh Pooh!" And, like me, she was rushed to the hospital with appendicitis. Sure enough, under the doll's shirt was her scar.

Many people visited from my parish. My friend Jim, the Unitarian minister, and my old friend Diana whom I had known since second grade drove three hours to see me. Tons of cards were sent with little notes, about sixty from my parish, which I taped all around my hospital room and at home when I was recuperating.

Judy worried about me. She was exhausted, too, fielding calls from my family and tending to me in addition to her own patients. When she looked closely at me with her serious doctor demeanor, I felt panicky. My lungs were clogged, so she sent in a physical therapist to pound on my back. The nurse warned me that I needed to do better blowing into their little plastic breathing apparatus: "The ninety-year-olds are getting more motion into these balls than you are." Living on Cape Cod, one doesn't accrue aging credentials until well after eighty.

Lying in the hospital bed, my worries were accentuated. My membership interview with the AAPC was coming up. My presenter lived in Maine. I called her from my hospital bed, trying to come up with some alternative. I wasn't quite in my right mind. I had labored for three years to go from Pastoral Counselor in Training to Member and another five to interview for Fellow level in the AAPC. I hated waiting, but there was nothing I could do but wait for the next review.

Recuperating from a ruptured appendix was slow; I lost weight and felt weak. Finally, in late November, I was back at church preaching. Judy attended and sat in front of a couple of parishioners. Since I was not "out" to most of the congregation, many members missed the opportunity of knowing her until ten years later when we returned and joined the church. Judy reported to me the whispers of the two concerned women, "There she is. She looks so pale and thin." I preached on the "wounded healer," inspired by Henri Nouwen's book.

I told my congregation that day that a nightmare can become a healing of body, mind, and spirit. I learned to trust God and others in a deeper way. The lectionary Epistle reading that day was from Romans: "Let no debt remain outstanding, except the continuing debt to love one another." (Romans 13:8, NIV)

I ended the sermon saying: "Each day of our lives we are challenged to be all that we can be in the light of God's call toward mutual love. God accepts us as both a wounded people as well as a people who are available to bind the wounds of others. It is often our acceptance of our own vulnerability in communion with others that instructs us in the very real presence of God's love."

THIRTY-FOUR

Abide with Me

Where do you hear what I am saying in your own center and can let
something grow in you that might be something very different than
what can grow in me; So that my words are more a space with which
you can come into touch with something that is uniquely yours.

—Henri Nouwen, talk given at Harvard Divinity School

"Abide in me, and I in you" (John 15:4, ESV), Jesus said in John's Gospel, which was the theme of the talk I attended by theologian and priest Henri Nouwen at Harvard Divinity School. Probably more than any other spiritual writer, Nouwen helped me imagine the nature of my ministry. What a privilege to be in his humble generous presence. Gesturing widely with his arms, he spoke in his clear Dutch accent of abiding as being at home with, being intimate with, sharing deeply with, finding joy in what is uniquely ours.

One afternoon at a nursing home I visited, a group of elders gathered to sing hymns. When it was time to leave, the melody lingered on. As I prepared to enter the room of my parishioner, I felt guided by a nurse wheeling a man back to his room as she hummed the hymn, "Abide with Me":

Swift to its close ebbs out life's little day;
earth's joys grow dim; its glories pass away;
change and decay in all around I see;
O thou who changest not, abide with me.

Mr. Tibbets was a retired lawyer who had shared poetry and his philosophy of life with me. He was now in the late stages of Parkinson's disease. His verbal ability was gone, but with God's help, I could abide with him still. The nurse who intoned the hymn did not know that day how she was an instrument of grace. Isn't that true of the many healers who make themselves available day in and day out?

I cherished visiting those educated women born at the end of the nineteenth century. Their ramblings left me a legacy in the course of the ebb and flow of pastoral encounters.

The day I visited Marian Morse. Still vibrant at ninety-nine years, she lay in bed reading a thick historical biography. She struggled putting on her hearing aids after I came in the room.

"As long as I can see you I will keep talking," she said with a twinkle, giving me permission to leave her room at the convalescent home.

A retired teacher, she had dedicated her life to bringing knowledge and opportunity to young adults. During the Depression years she worked in Florida to found community colleges that were affordable. I loved hearing her resonant voice, cultured yet warm. She deepened my appreciation for language. I had heard this voice before in other women in the parish, also in their nineties, who in their privileged youth attended schools like Radcliff, Smith, and Mt. Holyoke.

"I went to the library and found this book we spoke of last time," I said as I sat down in a chair next to her bed. Her room was furnished with her own bureau and desk and other keepsakes creating a warm, Victorian atmosphere. She looked over the book with interest.

"Now don't let me forget to return it to you so you can take it back to the library. Don't be awed by age."

Wow, I thought. How does she know I am awed by age?

I could hear my mother's voice, "Be nice, respect old people, someday you'll be old." I remember at age six meeting the oldest woman in my neighborhood. The day my family moved in to 46 Pleasantdale Road, Mrs. Hamaty, a large-boned peasant woman dressed in black, strode across the street. My father rolled down the window of our blue Plymouth. She peered in at me and said, "You're a nice-a girl. I will bring you candy and look after you."

A native of Beirut, she was a personage in our neighborhood. Looking out our front window, we could see her seated on the brick steps in front of her house, smoking cigarettes. "Stop smoking," my mother repeatedly told her. Yet my mother would hand me a carton of cigarettes to wrap up for her Christmas present. Mrs. Hamaty often called out to me as she saw me walking home from school: "Anne, come over. I have something for you." She would place a warm bowl of food in my hands to take home topped with a piece of Syrian bread. At that time, it wasn't available in supermarkets as only the Syrian kids brought pita bread to school. Under the bread might be lamb and rice, grape leaves or kibbe, my favorite dish of lamb and cracked wheat. My mother loved to recall the story of our great uncle ZiMichel, another old country personage. On one of his visits, he walked across the street, bent down in front of Mrs. Hamaty. He didn't have to bend far as he was short like all the men in my father's family. ZiMichel looked up at her face to see if she was really a woman.

Carmela Hamaty had one grown son, Mike, who lived with her. During snow storms and in frigid weather she'd be outside shoveling snow and warming up her son's car before he went off to work for the Veterans Administration. Her large coarse feet had only thongs for protection, what my mother called ziggies.

Johnny looked out the window on those cold snowy days and exclaimed, "Look, Ma, she's warming her son's car. When are you going to do that for me?"

"Over my dead body," chortled my mother.

Mrs. Hamaty's husband died when we first moved into the neighborhood. Three years later, my father died. She was quite fond of my father, as many people were who knew him. My mother waited a few days to break the news to her. As my mother recounted the story to me: "I dreaded telling Mrs. Hamaty about your father's death. When I crossed the street to tell her she screamed and began pulling her hair out. The neighbors ran out to see what the matter was, all trying to calm her down." Irish neighbors were unaccustomed to great displays of emotion and wanted to protect my mother. Mrs. Hamaty expressed grief freely as did her ancestors in Biblical times. Mrs. Hamaty abides in my memory, sitting on the stoop of her brick stairs like a grandmother, smoking and watching out for me as I rushed home from school. When my mother acted sternly toward me, Mrs. Hamaty would wave her hand down, a fed-up look on her face, "Ah, Anne's a nice-a girl!"

As my relationship with Marian Morse developed at the Orleans Convalescent Home, I was moved beyond awe in her presence. I told her about my passion for art. I brought in prints of my work from Castle Hill, where I went each summer to study and paint. She looked closely at my work, struck by its expressiveness. She announced: "I know the ministry is a noble profession, but don't neglect your art." On her 100th birthday, I filled her room with my paintings. A couple weeks later she died.

Marian's cousin Dorothy Goodell, also in her nineties, had the same unique manner and voice. I always visited Dorothy in the late afternoon, so I could join her for a glass of sherry and a piece of shortbread. The last time I saw her, I admired her blue flowers. She then recited Whittier's poem "Hyacinths for the Soul."

If thou of fortune be bereft,
and in thy store there be but left
two loaves, sell one, and with the
dole, buy hyacinths to feed thy soul.

After entrancing me with her stories, charm, and sherry, she'd pretend to seriously lament the fact that she could not be an orthodox or proper Congregationalist.

It was almost impossible for me to get out of the room when I visited another Dorothy, Miss Littlefield, the French professor who kept forgetting who I was. "I had a nice conversation with a woman psychologist who came to see me the other day," she'd say as I sat near her. When I told her that the woman psychologist probably was me, she responded with amusement and grace. "Well, that's fine," she laughed, not skipping a beat.

The past was infinitely more fascinating than the present, as Miss Littlefield told detailed stories of her trips with students to the Sorbonne and her meeting with the psychoanalyst Otto Rank. I was familiar with Otto Rank and his theories about art and psychology as my muse, Anaïs Nin, had written extensively about her psychoanalysis with him in her diaries. A strong-minded independent woman, Dorothy took great pleasure in telling me that she could not be psychoanalyzed by Rank. Dorothy implied that she was too tough and smart to be figured out by his analysis. I believed her, doubting that anyone would have had the nerve to analyze Miss Littlefield.

I heard a taped interview that Charlie Rose did with David Habersham. They were speaking about his career as a journalist. David said:

> You start out and think you're doing this because of your career; it's a good assignment. Then you realize, "I'm sixty-two," and you begin to take stock and see how it's changed you and affected your life. You realize it's not just a story. Your willingness to listen has enhanced you and made you larger. Remember in the seventies when we were getting into vegetarianism and we said: "You are what you eat." Maybe in journalism, you are who you interview.

Toward the end of my position at the Federated Church, my stepfather Tony became very ill. After a brief hospital stay, his doctor transferred him to a skilled nursing center where he died within a couple of weeks. My mother didn't want him home, feeling he needed too much care. I suspect she also didn't want to witness another husband die in her bedroom. Later I wished we had called in Hospice, but I didn't have the knowledge then, nor was Tony willing to go to a hospital specializing in end of life, as it frightened him. I gave the eulogy at his Catholic parish, and Ken from the Orleans church came to Boston to sing a solo.

I held ambivalent feelings about leaving the Federated Church as I saw opportunities to extend my visitation work as well as establish a pastoral counseling and spiritual development program there, but my position was just interim. Finding a ministry on Cape Cod to match my gifts continued to be difficult as was not being able to come out with the confidence of keeping my job. When I got an opportunity to become a Hospice Chaplain, I was somewhat relieved to leave parish work for the second time.

The week I began my training for Hospice I received news that my mother had cancer. Her doctor had found evidence of melanoma in the oddest place: her vagina. For years she warned Johnny he would get skin cancer if he didn't stop lying in the sun on weekends at Santa Monica beach. When he told our cousin about my mother's condition, she said incredulously, "How could that happen?" Johnny cracked, "She stood on her head in the backyard."

I had read in seminary of the Boston study that found that widows often come down with a major illness within a year of their spouse's death. I felt sorry for my mother having to deal with cancer in such a place of discomfort and privacy. Understandably, my mother wanted only me to accompany her to the hospital for surgery. I had trouble tracking down the surgeon after the first operation, and I took a dislike to him when we met. He told me in a cold succinct way that he thought he had gotten all the cancer but unfortunately had to do a lot of cutting in this vulnerable place. My mother healed quickly but she now had to deal with urinary incontinence. A couple additional surgeries were done to try to improve this condition, but they seemed to make it worse.

Entering Hospice ministry at the time of my mother's illness made my visitations to the dying even more poignant. Many times patients didn't come into Hospice until they were already close to death. Each Tuesday I opened our team meeting with a meditation for the staff and a prayer for those who had died that week. We talked about our patients and our feelings. I often got to know the family more than the patient, especially if the patient was close to death. I learned not to be afraid of being with a person who was dying and to recognize the signs and the timing of the last weeks or days. Since healing was no longer about medical cures and faith was no longer about bargaining with God, the intimate yet ordinary moments of being with the person mattered tremendously.

"Harry, put the bird away. The chaplain is coming." We gathered around the coffee table in their apartment in a small housing development. Cathy was suffering from cancer. The room was enveloped in cigarette smoke, so much so that I had to remove all my clothes and hang them in the garage when I got home. I feared flying birds ever since early childhood when my dad took me to the zoo. In spite of these predicaments, I witnessed the most poignant Our Father prayed as we all held hands over the table . . . Give us this day, our daily bread . . .

Judy observed that Hospice workers have a "transparent" look about them. "You are becoming that way too," she told me. Maybe it was the selflessness of the work. Maybe it was entering into the numinous transition between life and death with another human being.

Three stories describe my year as a Hospice Chaplain—the easiest visit, the hardest visit, and the most touching visit. One day I sat on the couch with a woman in her seventies. Immediately, we got engaged in conversation with no small talk. She told me she had lived well and meaningfully and had fulfilled her last wish with a trip to Australia. The travel poster hung above her. Later in the visit, she confided that she had had a troubling dream the night before and was tired. I suggested she try doing guided imagery with me. I led her to a special place, and eventually she went off to sleep. I quietly left her home. Two days later I learned she had died peacefully.

Another time I was called to see a woman at a nursing center. She was around forty; her leg had been amputated, and the stench in the room was unbearable. Her only kin, her sister, was with her. She asked her sister for a Coke and then added to get one for me. That small kind act stayed with me alongside the suffering of being with her in that room. After she died I visited her sister, and together we went over to the beach, said prayers, and flung her ashes into the water.

Religion for many hospice patients was important. I found myriad ways to connect with their beliefs. Sometimes, though, religion was a stumbling block, especially if the person had guilt from their childhood faith or if they didn't see themselves as religious. I had no problem with that, but I did have a problem with a fundamentalist man. In my work with fundamentalist clients, I have found them to have a strong core of shame and guilt. When it is possible for them to let go of these shameful feelings, their beliefs become less rigid, along with their personalities. My own counter-transference, that is my own feelings of being with a fundamentalist, evoked fear and shame in me. Fundamentalists are often homophobic and feeling-phobic. On my first visit with Chuck, I noticed his organ. He told me the organ was his prized possession. He played a simple piece and gave me one of his music books. Thank God, I could minister to him with music. A week later, our team, comprised of his nurse, social worker, and I, visited his tiny cottage with a birthday cake. I played my guitar and we all sang. A few weeks later he could no longer live alone, so we moved him to Hospice House. I requested his organ be moved and it was! A few days before he died I visited with my guitar. He was too weak to get out of bed, so I played for him and sang old hymns. One of the nurses came into the room and joined with me, "Softly and tenderly, Jesus is calling . . . Come Home, you who are weary come home."

The saddest story during my year working for Hospice happened to one of our very own. A nurse was driving back from Provincetown after having seen a patient. The snow blanketed Route 6 and her car skidded off the road. She died, leaving several young children. Her memorial service was held at St. David's in Yarmouth. I was asked to play guitar and sing to her six-year-old son the song his mother sang to him: "You are my sunshine . . ."

THIRTY-FIVE

L-Shaped House

That autumn we braced ourselves for layoffs at Hospice. Ever since I had the job, there was always the threat of cuts whenever the census went down. To our surprise, my nurse supervisor, Pam, received the pink slip first; her parting words to me were: "I just got my real estate license. I will find you a new home for Healthsigns."

While I valued the experience of being a chaplain at Hospice, it also took a toll on my body and emotions. I didn't like long drives in the wide Upper Cape area finding patients' homes and the insecurity of not knowing what to expect when I entered the home. I often felt hungry, tempted to stop at every little eating place I came across, and there weren't many. I looked forward to joining our healthcare team every week for the mutual support and guidance so needed in this work.

One day I spoke on the phone with my counselor as I looked out my window on a cold snowy day. I was mentally preparing myself for the layoff while feeling some guilt. Pat said to me in a compassionate tone, "Anne, you don't have to do this work any longer. It is alright."

Around Christmas time, I received news of my lay-off and left later that day. Six months later I had an opportunity to return when one of the other chaplains retired, but by that time I had already moved on, focused on my new home and revitalizing Healthsigns. Pam had found us the perfect L-shaped home in the historic district of Yarmouth Port.

Judy disliked change and whined that I was taking her away from her favorite beach. The new house had a quaint English garden with continually blooming flowers (my favorite, the poppy) and many unique trees to entice Judy, the budding gardener. Wall-to-wall book cases in the Williamsburg green living room brought joy to me, along with an upstairs room for an art studio and a sweet cottage next door for Healthsigns.

After we passed papers we drove over to the house on April 1st. There had been a surprise snowstorm overnight so when we arrived the snow piled up from the plows blocked the driveway. Out of nowhere appeared a large round figure in a bright yellow jacket like fishermen wear with a snow blower. He was clearing our driveway! We got out of the car to thank him. He put out his hand and said: "Hi, I am Paul your new neighbor. Welcome to the neighborhood."

Our friends and Healthsigns board members helped us move our ton of books and record albums: Pam, our realtor, her husband Loyall, Judy and Dave Rogers. It was April of 1997. We got soaked in the pouring rain as we formed an assembly line moving the stuff through our front door.

We wanted everyone to come to dinner at the Aardvark restaurant a mile down the street, but we needed dry clothes. So we took clothes from Dave's truck that were on their way to the thrift shop. A motley crew celebrating in the back room of the inn, we drank champagne, laughed at ourselves, and toasted to our new home.

In our Christmas letter we counted our blessings of 1997: L-Shaped house on Old King's Highway, an English garden, and ghosts of a minister and doctor who had lived here nearly 200 years ago. Eating on Rte. 6 A: Aardvark, Old Yarmouth Inn, Inaho Japanese restaurant, and Jack's Outback. (Jack was an institution of the neighborhood. A tall taciturn humorous Yankee, he surprised me the first week I moved in by calling out *Arrivederci* as I left his restaurant.) Our Healthsigns cottage added a special garden in front designed by Dave. A resident chipmunk loved to visit the garden. We named her Julian, after the medieval English Saint Julian of Norwich, who declared, "All Shall be Well, All Manner of Things Shall be Well."

The house is one of several antiques on the National Historic Register on Old King's Highway, built in 1820 and added to over the years. We contributed our part too, privileged to explore the delicate line between past and present. Thanks to the painstaking research of Aunt Ethel, our friend Margaret's aunt, we know something about the many inhabitants who lived and loved and died here. Though the house is ours now, we understand that one day we too will pass it on.

Just a bit along 6A sits a tiny white house called the Friday Club. The Friday Club began in the early 1900s when a group of church ladies from the First Congregational Church came together to socialize and raise money for scholarships for young people. About once a month on a Saturday morning, the Friday Club opens its doors as all of us gathered outside rush in to buy delicious homemade pies for Thanksgiving, casseroles in the winter, and strawberry shortcake in June.

Every other Friday I cross the Old King's Highway to join seven others in our own Friday group. We don't call ourselves a club; we began as a group of practicing professionals to provide supervision and training for a pastoral counseling trainee. Several years passed and we evolved into something else, trading in our outward-looking perspectives and theories for our inward leanings for the calls we find in our middle years and beyond, for the issues of the day that move us in our search for a faith that sustains us. Our religious backgrounds include Jewish, Protestant, and Catholic traditions. As we gather in Annie's house for coffee and muffins, by the fire in winter, we bring prayers, poems, and meditations. In time we have come to know what each of us values and we help that to flourish. We are all wash-a-shores on Cape Cod, most of us having lived in cities where we had access to universities, cultural and religious diversity. Yet we are entranced by the magic of Cape Cod.

Judy and I took a mini-vacation to Land's End Inn in Provincetown. We decided to invite the Friday group to join us. The topic for our discussion was place. What is your sense of place? I opened with a Renaissance piece I played on the guitar. Many people brought poetry to share: Art brought a poem by his favorite poet, Robert Frost; Marilyn read from her Jewish prayer book; Judy read "Dover Beach"; Mike, the naturalist among us, read a poem by our Cape Cod treasure, Mary Oliver. Looking out the rounded window toward the ocean at the end of the land on the tip of the Cape, the words he read penetrated my soul. I knew then that place for me is located in the heart-soul connection, the place that opens the heart so it can find its home in the soul's belly.

I revisited my request that I had initiated three years previously for standing through the United Church of Christ. To my surprise, while meeting with the interim Associate Minister, he proposed I become part of the denomination through my ministry at Healthsigns. I was thrilled to make this "marriage" work between my vision and the church. The committee that had rejected my request had a new chair who apologized to me for the previous review and acknowledged the fine work I had done as a pastor and counselor on the Cape. A year later I was invited to become part of their board, which I did for several years. I felt that my role was to not only bring a pastoral counseling perspective but also to watch carefully for biases as we reviewed ministers who sought standing in the U.C.C. I never became a comfortable "talker" in committee meetings, but I spoke up when I felt my voice was most important, often the lone voice.

I envisioned new possibilities for Healthsigns by forming a group of healing and counseling practitioners. One of our most fun events was Healing for the Healers. Healthcare professionals and ministers were invited to meet with area congregations for dinner and entertainment. Judy Rogers cooked up huge pots of vegetarian soup, matzo ball chicken soup, and fresh rolls.

My discovery of the book *The Artist's Way*, a kind of twelve-step program for creative types, became a godsend for me to help me value myself as an artist and to support other creative types. Practicing the Artist's Way led to "good directions" in my own life; what author Julia Cameron calls GOD: good orderly direction.

Over the course of ten years, I facilitated many Artist's Way groups through Healthsigns. Our participants included writers, painters, healers, therapists, musicians, and retired people. We also had a group for children at the Lutheran church, pastored by Healthsigns board member Rev. Dr. Jane O'Hara Shields with special craft projects and lunches from cultures around the world.

Meanwhile, I was urged to speak to my former parishioners at the Federated Church in Orleans. The church had formed a committee to explore becoming an Open and Affirming Church, a policy of welcome to lesbians and gay people in the United Church of Christ. While there were hardly any gay people in the congregation, there were parents and friends who felt strongly about inclusion. There were also many who didn't understand why gay people needed a "special welcome" along with others who could not "affirm" the lives of gays and lesbians. The committee believed I would make a difference by coming out since I had been loved and respected when I ministered there four years earlier. The church had begun the "Q&A" process soon after I left, but the congregation was still not ready.

As I was no longer threatened by ties to my American Baptist denomination and since my Privilege of Call in the United Church of Christ was to Healthsigns and not to a local church, I had achieved some safety and freedom. I accepted the committee's invitation to speak with the congregation.

Anxious but confident, I was amazed to see the Vestry full. They kept bringing in folding chairs. My friend Phil Mitchell, a retired pastor, introduced me. Phil used to get my name mixed up and call me Irene. He did so again that night, probably nervous like the rest of us. His round, warm face reddened, and he said, " I don't know why I do that." All those vowels in my full name, perhaps he was trying to say my last name first and pronounce it right.

I was on fire that night, walking from one side of the room to the other, using my hands, inviting questions, maintaining good eye contact as when I preach, noticing the smiles on many faces and a few men literally burying their heads on their chests. While I didn't find it easy to speak extemporaneously, when I was passionate about a subject and when it involved promoting justice and understanding, I rose to the occasion.

I told my former parishioners about my growing up, my coming out, even my experience with the Italian Lesbians. "And what do you think we did, the Italian Lesbians, when we got together?" I challenged them. "Eat!" they shouted back, and the room broke into laughter. When one genuinely concerned middle-aged lady in the back asked me, "What can I do to understand, to help?" I shot back "Invite me for dinner!" More laughter. Our friend John, whose wife was Judy's patient, approached me after the meeting. I knew he was part of the group against becoming Open and Affirming. Yet I made an impression on him too that night as he told me, "You ought to be a stand-up comedian."

There were moments of tension, especially when the head deacon, Bob, the chair of the search committee that had hired me, stood up and said in a rather desperate voice: "But we love you, Anne. Don't you know that?" "Yes, Bob, but love has to be just. You can't love someone and treat them differently. If you had known of my sexual orientation, I doubt you would have hired me." He sat down, looking deflated.

There was a lot of fear from the few who were most threatened by the idea of sexuality coming to the "church near you." One of the women involved in the Welcoming Committee at the church told me of the ridiculous idea that "All the gays from Provincetown would appear in the parking lot of the church one day." Linda said, disgustedly, "Sure, they can't wait to come to our church!" A man of large stature, part of the country club group, hobbled up to me a few months later and said, "You know you turned me around 180 degrees that night you spoke."

That night was a watershed moment for me. I knew I had to continue to help individuals and congregations "get it" and open their minds and hearts to LGBTQ people and their allies. A year later, Healthsigns organized an interfaith conference on Welcoming Congregations. Jews, Methodists, Catholics, Congregationalists, Unitarians, Quakers, Episcopalians and others worshiped together and discussed ways to show further acceptance for LGBTQ persons. We grew our own movement up and down Cape Cod, forming lasting friendships over many years.

Now as so many aspects of my life had beautifully come together: art, ministry, community, and our new home, there was just one thing lacking . . . a dog!

Dr. Duchy

The dog is a gentleman; I hope to go to his heaven, not man's.

—attributed to Mark Twain

For years I told Judy I wanted a dog. She repeatedly said no. I felt ambivalent myself, as it was so long since I'd had a dog. I worried something bad might happen. I had had to part with two dogs because I didn't have an adequate home for them. Now that we had a large house on Cape Cod with a yard, and I worked next door to my home, it seemed the perfect time.

But what kind of dog? I discovered Poodle Rescue of New England. I could help rescue a dog! Also, poodles are smart and non-allergenic. I heard that poodles rank number two after border collies in intelligence, which would be ideal for helping me in my therapy work as a pastoral counselor. Judy said defiantly, "It's me or the dog." I took the gamble and replied, "the dog." After twenty years with Judy, I knew she doth protest too much.

The Provincetown florist was part of Poodle Rescue of New England. In October of 2000 I timidly entered her shop to inquire about adoption. She gave me the contact information. I filled out the two page application and mailed it in. The weekend before the New Year of 2001 was bitterly cold. A call came in from a poodle foster home in Milton. "I have a seven-month-old black male miniature poodle. Would you like to come see him?"

I paused and said, "I wrote on my application that I wanted a female."

"Yes, I know," the voice answered, "but he has a gentle personality; he is not an alpha dog. I think you'll like him."

"I will be there on New Year's Day," I said. Judy agreed to accompany me, though she was still dead set against a dog. Her tone became, "It will be your dog."

An Asian-American woman named Evelyn opened the door and welcomed us to her home. Two huge beautiful standard poodles were scampering around; a tiny jet-black poodle with a white-and-mocha-striped beard was playing with them. His body was the size of their heads.

Evelyn offered us tea and we talked. She said we were fortunate to get a puppy. All of his veterinary care was complete. Did I want to hold him? She put him on my lap. There was something sad about this little creature. He melted into my lap and went to sleep. Evelyn asked if Judy wanted to hold him. "No," Judy replied stone faced.

As the puppy continued to cling to me, I knew I would adopt him. "What is his name?" I asked. "Luigi was his name," she said. "Two young boys used to visit him in a pet shop in Newton. He was there a long time. A man brought him home for his wife, but she preferred a Chihuahua, so he took him back. The boys begged their mother to take him out of the pet shop; she agreed, provided he would go to Poodle Rescue for adoption. Around Christmas time they saved their allowance, got him out, and brought him to their home for a week. Then he came here. We got him ready for adoption and named him Flying Dutchman based on his unsettled history."

Before we left with our new poodle, Evelyn gave us a sweet blue sweater with "VIP" on the back, along with a rubber chicken toy from the boys. Boston was colder than the Cape, and the sidewalks were a sheet of ice. Since I usually drive, Judy needed to hold the dog. The Flying Dutchman was shaking, so Judy put him inside her coat and held him until we made it safely home.

I could see some early signs of connection developing between my puppy and Judy. "He's not coming in the bedroom," she declared. I agreed to keep him in the kitchen. During the night, we woke to his cries. I went to comfort him. He was sleeping with the little chicken toy.

That morning Judy told me her dream. "I dreamed the dog was sitting erect and graceful in a lotus position. Looking up at me, he said with a Chinese accent, 'I am eighty-two-year-old.' I wonder if he could be my Chinese grandfather?"

"Yes, I am sure he could," I said quickly, silently hoping this might contribute to the bonding process.

After another sleepless night with the dog in the kitchen, Judy began to soften, and he graduated to our bedroom. I ran out Tuesday between clients and bought two beds for him: one for my office and one for the house. Each night before he went to bed, he came around to each side of the bed and pushed himself up to the edge with his front paws to greet Judy and me. I don't think he did this in a particular order, almost careful not to play favorites. "I think he is saying goodnight to us," I told Judy. "Yes," she was clearly impressed. "Can you believe it? Have you ever seen a dog do that before?"

My clients loved him, and we talked a lot about dogs for a few weeks. One of my counselees chided me for not calling him by name. I wasn't sure what to call him yet. We liked Luigi and figured the boys came from an Italian family. Nevertheless, shouldn't he have a French name?

Flying Dutchman was too long and now that he had a permanent home, it didn't exactly fit. I decided on Duchy, as in the Duchy of Brittany, Anjou, etc. It seemed a proper balance between sophisticated and winsome. At Healthsigns we also called him Dr. Duché.

After a couple of months, Duchy graduated again, this time to a permanent place at the end of our sleigh bed. By now Judy was crazy about Duchy, walking him every day and meeting all our neighbors. After only a week, her colleagues noticed a change in her. "Dr. R, you look so happy!" a nurse exclaimed. Dr. R even told a depressed patient to get a dog, and away she went for the "canine cure."

Duchy followed me to work, past the boxwood bushes surrounding our English garden, out the white picket gate, up the path past the newly designed Healthsigns garden to my cottage office. He reminded me of the movie I saw in Psych 101 of the ducks that followed the psychologist like their mother. Soon he knew each of my clients and how to respond to them; whom to lick in the face, whom to curl up next to, and whom to leave alone. Many times he consoled a tearful person. He was particularly attentive to the teenagers I saw. Hardly anyone came in distressed anymore.

He especially loved the two "dog biscuit ladies;" he would sit, lie down, and dance, shaking his head from side to side. Sometimes he'd fall asleep in his bed during a session and let out a moan if someone was carrying on angrily. Duchy also groaned if Judy and I talked in bed too long at night when it was time to go to sleep.

When Duchy was still a puppy, a new client Tim came in for counseling. He was referred by his wife who threatened to separate if he didn't change his ways. A middle-aged curmudgeon, he told me during our first session, "If I knew you were a minister I would never have set foot in your office." While I grew fond of Tim, Duchy really tipped the scales. The two of them spent the first few minutes of every session playing. Tim said, "My dog and cat don't receive me like this. He's got too much personality for a dog."

One day when Judy was out walking Duchy, Tim came in looking concerned: "Where is he?"

"Oh, he's out with Judy," I said.

"Well, I am only going to pay you for half. We males have to stick together."

After a couple of years, Tim said, "I am coming for myself not for my wife." I must admit that while I will take some credit for changing his perspective, Duchy deserves the most credit.

Judy and I spent a lot of quality time with Duchy when he was a puppy. His coat was not healthy so we got a natural healthy formula dog food and mixed it with flax seed oil. To help him relax and feel safe, I would hold him to my breast, and we would fall asleep together. We took him to puppy class. A dog trainer came out to the house and saw he was withdrawn. He never barked. "Just build his confidence first before formal training," he advised us.

One day when my friend Kula came over to do some counseling supervision with me, she brought her huge shepherd Q to meet Duchy. Q was trained by the Monks of New Skete and worked with Kula doing therapy. Unexpectedly, he lunged at Duchy; Duchy barked and ran like hell. From that day on, Duchy barked if anyone came to the door or if he heard a neighborhood dog barking. Kula came to see me about once a month and gave the Pasha, her nickname for Duchy, a biscuit before we began our time together. One day she put her suede gloves on top of her briefcase on the kitchen floor. Duchy snatched the gloves and put a big hole in one glove before I caught him. I said to Kula that I would get her a new pair at Filene's, which I did. In fact, Judy and I established a Duchy fund for other such casualties, which included two pairs of gloves and a pink-laced panty stolen from an overnight guest. When Kula returned a couple of months later, Duchy went into his basket and brought Kula her old glove. Who said dogs don't remember?

Duchy got himself into trouble a lot in the first two years we had him. At our Welcoming Congregations planning meeting, he took the toothbrush out of the Unitarian minister's purse and paraded through our living room with it hanging out of his mouth. He pulled the telephone out of the socket in my office and got the wires caught around his neck. He ran squealing around the cottage with the phone following him; I followed shrieking after him until I finally untangled it before he could choke. Then I sat on the couch, held him for a long time, and called Judy to tell her what happened. Another day, he swallowed a paper clip, so we rushed him to the nearest hospital, an hour away. The vet was able to remove it from his stomach with a clothes hanger-type tool.

Not long after that, I got a call from Judy while I was at a clergy retreat. "I think you better come home. Duchy is sick. He can't walk." We rushed back to the same hospital, but the vet we liked was not in that day. A younger vet did an x-ray and said he couldn't find anything, but he would put him on steroids. Judy was upset, and I could tell she was about to get very angry. "I would never give steroids to a patient without a diagnosis!" she said, and stormed out leaving me to deal with the perplexed vet.

We carried Duchy out and drove back to the Cape. "I have an idea Judy. Let's call Loyall." Loyall, the husband of my former Hospice supervisor, was an animal lover and chiropractor. I had recalled he was privately seeing a few animals at his home in his spare time. I felt relieved when Loyall picked up the phone. "Bring him right over," he said kindly.

Loyall put the x-ray on his projector and said, "I see at the tip of his spine a small place that is causing this problem. I have a special instrument that has been used successfully with horses." He used it to touch several pressure points on Duchy's spine; miraculously, Duchy stood up and walked. The next day Duchy slept soundly in the kitchen with Daddy-O cooing by his side. (I had named Judy Daddy-O since I seemed obviously to be Duchy's mommy.) The next day he rose up and walked; one more treatment and he completely recovered.

Our friends presented us with a photo of Judy holding Duchy with me, my hand on his back, at the water's edge. The wooden black frame forms the word, Family. Duchy made us a family and remained our loyal son for eighteen years.

After Duchy received his "Good Canine Diploma," which I hung in my office's waiting room, I took him to agility training, another way to boost his confidence and socialize him. After a couple of classes, we realized he was a people pleaser and couldn't care less about competition. One class was made up of women with little Shetland collies, who seemed bred for serious competition. The collies looked straight ahead while running up the ramps and through the tunnels and hoops. Like the students who got all As in school, they had their eyes on the prize. Not

Duchy; maybe he was taking after his mom too much. He greeted the owners of the collies, but he was distracted by all the excitement in the ring. He was terrified of losing his balance on the platform that moved, as well as running through a dark smelly tunnel. I put treats at either end of the tunnel, stooping down to look through to him, calling him, begging him, until finally he made it out the other side.

Judy didn't come to the second agility class; she often got nervous herself. "Stop pushing him. He's just a little dog," she'd yell at me. When she came to the next class and saw him jump through the high hoop, she had tears of pride in her eyes. The woman who didn't want a dog.

THIRTY-SEVEN

Icons

Fishermen know that the sea is dangerous and the storm terrible, but they have never found these dangers sufficient to keep them ashore.

—Vincent van Gogh

At St. Edmund's Retreat Center in Mystic, Connecticut, I had this dream: Peering out my window, I saw water coming onto the island, heading for the retreat house and taking down trees and structures in its way. I ran out of the room, but it was quiet except for the shadowy figures of persons that I could not cry out to, reminiscent of my childhood dreams of losing my mother.

Spending a week "writing" an icon of the Archangel Michael was pulling at my nerves; the winds were blowing fiercely; the rain was sweeping against my window. But the island wasn't flooding. It was just a small hurricane on the island. The radio predictions and the intense concentration of working on my first icon had fueled my anxious active imagination.

My life was changing again in 2003. I needed a sabbatical, which the Healthsigns Board supported and helped with programming while I was away. I had never stopped counseling for more than a couple of weeks at a time over many years, and I was exhausted. I worried that Duchy would be sad to give up his work with me. Yet I felt drawn to get back to my creative work and needed a prolonged artist's date. Why did God give me so many different gifts without there being enough time? It had taken so long to develop them given the many life obstacles I had to contend with.

On New Year's Eve I pondered: "How does one find Sabbath time?" Answering my own question, I knew: "Make an intention to change. Decide what not to do. Meditate on letting go. Schedule a time of retreat. Set up solitary time for meditation, art and music. Be with others who honor Sabbath. Move from human time to God time." I loved planning my sabbatical. At last an opportunity to live more fully as an artist. As usual, I had more ideas than days to do them.

At the end of June, I spent time in Cambridge with my former teacher Katie Cannon, taking a preaching/writing workshop. I hadn't seen her in almost twenty years. Katie said in her usual persuasive manner: "There are two kinds of days: good days and days when I am not doing the work. On those days I need to write." In July I studied classical guitar at the National Guitar Workshop. In August I took my first memoir workshop at the Blue Hills Writing Institute. Now I would learn to write an icon.

In the Orthodox tradition, prayer is the first step in "writing" an icon. The Eastern Orthodox believe it is God who writes the icon on our hearts. Instead of my usual thrashing around my art studio with loud music and van Gogh-like strokes, I quietly tried to master each step of the icon process: applying the clay and smoothing it out with fine sandpaper, blowing on the gold leaf to adhere it to the clay, using tiny brushes to highlight the robes and float the next set of colors over it, and then adding the second and third highlights. I didn't know what it was going to look like, so I had to trust the Russian youth who guided us through each step. The process took me from dark to light. The final step in making an icon is to place the white in the eyes and the white around the halo of the head. This is the "uncreated" light that only God makes. Archangel Michael is the first icon for a beginner in the Prosperon School, the icon that sits on the right side of the iconostasis in Orthodox churches.

Nick, the Italian stained glass teacher, all heart and sweetness, tiptoed into our studio and put his arm on my shoulder as I quietly worked, Orthodox chants playing in the background. Nick whispered, "This feels like heaven." And it does.

The Spirit of God flowed through me and through the work when I let go of my control. However, that proved quite a challenge. My descent into hell was swift. I was troubled, impatient. I picked up a terrible allergy at the center probably from mold. I said to myself, "I will never do this again!" My brush slipped and I muttered under my breath, "damn." Agnes, the bossy Catholic Vietnamese woman who shared my table, exuding patience and perfection in her painstaking dedication to icon-making, said playfully, "I heard that; that's not very holy."

I returned to my room and prayed to Michael: *Archangel Michael, protect me as my soul battles wounds of injustice and vulnerability. Build me a tree house safe from hurricanes that afflict my mind and trouble my spirit. Build me a tree house that grants me time where my body is a temple, my mind is a poet, my soul is an icon of God's love. Build me a tree house where my will becomes pure agency, my anger becomes righteous, my sorrows become transformed.*

Evening came. Our class had just feasted on a great meal. The priest in charge, a gourmet cook, saw to it that the food was well prepared with plenty to eat. I returned to the workshop and peeked in. Most of the participants had gone to their rooms to read or sleep. But there was Agnes working diligently at our table. Across the way at the next table, a woman in her eighties who came all the way from Mexico City, was also working. She was planning to build a chapel near her home for a Catholic religious order, and it would be filled with icons. I watched her blowing so hard on the clay that I worried she could have a heart attack. How did she have the stamina to keep going after a full day? I felt a bit ashamed at my inward complaints.

The next day I awoke renewed and focused. Finally, I am seeing the Archangel emerge from the floating process. Soon I will finish the highlights and then take my compass and carefully make a thin circle to place the white of the halo, and a dot for the white of each eye. It is finished. It is beautiful. Behold what God and I have done!

Usually, the finished icons were placed on the altar at Mass on Sunday mornings. I felt ambivalent about going to Mass because at St. Edmund's it is written in the worship bulletin that communion will not be offered to non-Catholics. I talked this over with a Lutheran minister from New York who had been writing icons for many years. We both felt badly about this rule, feeling it to be contrary to the will of Jesus Christ who invited all people to be part of his ministry. The sacrament was so central to the Mass that to deny the "bread of God for the people of God" was like inviting someone to your home and having them wait while you eat dinner in front of them. Can you imagine an Italian acting that way?

Fortunately, Agnes saved me from having to make a decision as to whether or not to stay for Mass. She had to catch an early plane out of Providence, and I agreed to drive her to the airport. Against my better judgment, I purchased from my teacher a piece of wood prepared with gesso, thereby inviting the next icon. Sure enough, a couple of years later I went to the lower east side of New York for a week to complete the icon, Archangel Gabriel, in the basement at the Russian Cathedral. I presented the icon of Gabriel to my mother who kept it on her hope chest next to her bed.

THIRTY-EIGHT

Crossing the Bridge

Not everything that is faced can be changed, but
nothing can be changed until it is faced.

—James Baldwin, *New York Times Book Review*, January 14, 1962

Our ministers' group of mostly retired men gathered for a monthly meeting. I have known these men for several years, and I value our history of time and our camaraderie.

One day the Spirit moved among us. Without being planned, stories flowed about an extraordinary time they shared when they answered the call as white pastors to be part of the Civil Rights struggle to end segregation. Phil began in his characteristic way with a personal story: "I was naïve, perhaps, thinking that going to Selma wasn't going to cause any controversy in the small rural town in New Hampshire where I was pastor. A deacon in the church came up to me and said, 'If you do this, I will not only resign as deacon but I will leave the church'." Phil, always warm-hearted and jovial, had heard Dr. King on the radio asking all pastors to come to Alabama to bear witness to the struggle for civil rights. Phil knew what he had to do in spite of his own leanings toward consensus. He drove to Selma and marched, not realizing, like many northerners, the intense danger, animosity and fear of the white southerners toward blacks. These deeply embedded attitudes erupted in torrents of hatred and violence toward northerners butting in to join the cause. Soon after Phil returned from Alabama, he got a surprise visit from the deacon, a letter in his hand. Phil nervously took the letter from the deacon who had been so angry. The letter was signed by the whole board of deacons. The Board commended Phil for the courageous action he took and pledged their full support.

As Phil recounted his story, our room grew even quieter as we felt and saw the emotion in his face. History is not merely a series of events but a human movement with potential for good or for ill. How often it is a convergence of both. These young pastors marched not only with their feet but with their souls carried by the forces of freedom in the face of oppression. And yet today our country is still divided.

The conversation continued as Gordon, seated to the left of Phil, pointed out that his church in black urban Cleveland had no doubts he must go. They practically pushed him out the door, and for all his passionate belief in the cause, when he crossed the bridge in Selma, he felt fear. Gordon, in his usual honest, engaging style said to the young black man next to him: "Aren't you afraid?" "No, because you are here with me," came the reply that disarmed his fears.

Crossing the bridge is the road we walk down when our defenses and pretenses are stripped away. Crossing the bridge to fight injustice is not a solitary affair. And when we take that step outside our secure homes, we are met by unimaginable forces. Forces embracing us allow us to remake goodness into courage; forces working against us lead us to turn evil thoughts into evil deeds.

Art, seated to the left of Gordon, could not hold his peace any longer. Slowly raising his arm he said: "Is it OK to have my turn now?" Art spoke slowly but with emphasis and passion:

"The elders in my Presbyterian Church were very much in favor of my going. There were crowds of people that were well managed by the black local leadership. At first, I couldn't understand why they told us to do exactly what they said and to disregard any other communications. Later, I witnessed attempts by others to send us to a nearby church to sleep with the intent to destroy the church. Even returning to New Jersey was dangerous; we were saved from getting on a plane with a bomb on it. None of this was reported in the press. In spite of the dangers and having to sleep outdoors, I wanted so badly to get to Montgomery and see Dr. King. Instead, I ended up sick and weak in St. Jude's Hospital. They took wonderful care of me, but I was, frankly, PO'd I couldn't make it to the rally. The nurse said to me: "You can't leave as long as we have your clothes.""

Throughout the conversations were memories of Dr. King. Bob, sitting to the left of me, recalls how moved he was to hear his roommate being filled with longing to return home to the south and help his people. He was praying for a leader to stimulate change in this country. It was the fifties. His roommate was Andrew Young.

Wells, at the far end of the table, remembered being in a limo with Martin Luther King, Jr., in the early years. He had forgotten the words that were spoken, but he remembered the beautiful shine on King's black shoes.

Bill proceeded to speak in his Scottish Presbyterian measured and kindly way:

I never spoke to my grandchildren about this. It is like we all have been through a common war, and now we are giving voice to what we saw. It is impossible to convey the feelings and pathos of those times. I was one of the guys in Selma who distributed food to the marchers, like Mrs. Viola Liuzzo who was murdered by the Klan. I too got close to Dr. King, but I am embarrassed to say I bumped into him and spilled coffee on his shiny black shoes. I was very apologetic. Dr. King was very gracious. I heard him deliver "I Have A Dream." Never have I heard such oratory! The segregationists were blaring "Bye, Bye Blackbird" as we went over the bridge. I cannot hear that song without remembering, without being overwhelmed by feelings.

I was just a kid in the sixties playing Dylan on my guitar and dreaming of change. But I came to know how truth bears a solitary long loneliness until you stretch over that bridge where there is a brother or sister ready to accompany you toward freedom, confident that you can save each other no matter what happens.

[top] My brother Johnny [bottom] Wedding vows

Legal Marriage

The Sixth Call: 2005

In the New Year, about eight months after marriage had become legal in Massachusetts, I declared, "We need to get married, Judy, before the state changes its mind." After twenty-five years together, I wanted a wedding celebration with all whom we held dear.

[top] Wedding guests [bottom] Duchy dressed for the occasion; wedding cake

THIRTY-NINE

Wedding Bells

Risk! Risk anything! Care no more for the opinions of others, for those voices. Do the hardest thing on earth for you. Act for yourself.

—Katherine Mansfield, *The Journal of Katherine Mansfield*

Begin to be now what you will be hereafter.

—William James

"WILL YOU MARRY US?" ASKED THE TWO WOMEN ONE AFTERNOON IN MY office.

"Yes," I replied. "Do you have a date?"

"Saturday," they smiled, slightly embarrassed. "Now we are ready to be among the first in Massachusetts to be legally wed."

"Saturday," I thought to myself. Not my usual way to prepare a couple, never mind myself, but these are extraordinary times. I trusted these women.

"OK, Saturday at your home. Let's meet again. We can email our ideas on the service."

I felt the excitement building between us.

"Oh, and you are welcome to bring your partner," whom they hadn't met yet, "and your dog," who was sitting there on the couch with them witnessing this whole amazing encounter.

Jean and Joan lived on a cove on the Lower Cape. Even though the month was May, it was a typical Cape Cod spring—cold and windy. Not being a hardy type, I was relieved to see a fire burning in their living room. Several women friends gathered; we formed a circle outside surrounded by pines overlooking the ocean. Duchy poodle was the only male present. The couple chose the readings and music for the service. I read the invocation by Diane Mariechild: "Each time the heart opens, the power of love is strengthened. In this way, strong relationships are gifts to the world." "I Have Dreamed," sung by Julie Andrews, followed and then the poem "Wild Geese" by Mary Oliver, our beloved Cape poet.

After the ceremony we went inside and warmed up. Friends had prepared a roast beef dinner, and a wedding cake was purchased by a friend who excitedly had rushed into a bakery in the Boston area that morning, asking for an "emergency wedding cake." After explaining the reason for the rush, the bakers gladly obliged.

Judy and I had watched on television the Constitutional Convention in Massachusetts for the duration of the debates on gay marriage. Never had the political process been so personal and so central to our lives and our future. During those exciting days, we rode a surfboard of feelings; surging with joy and pride one moment and plunging into anxiety and despair the next. I tracked every legislator from each district in the Commonwealth, cheering with the champions, growling at the deniers. Even after gay marriage was legal, another challenge presented itself—the law came up for repeal two years later. Fortunately, we were spared what would have been a travesty like the one in California where some couples became legal and others not.

That year, when same-sex marriage became legal in our state, we were in the process of couples therapy with Betsy Bishop. The presenting problem was the kitchen remodel. Judy and I had never tackled an alteration in our home demanding so many decisions leading to arguments. There weren't many areas of disagreement, but we were equally insistent on our own perspective. In years past, Judy didn't have such strong opinions regarding the house so I didn't know how to respond to her objections. Actually, I did respond, with anger. Besides her wondering why Formica was not good enough for the counter, she wanted to take down the fake wall in front of the chimney on which I had a painting. Since I hung my paintings anywhere I could find a wall, not easy in an old home, I coveted that space. Also, uncharacteristically, since I usually voted for change over Judy's conservatism, I feared what I might see behind that wall.

The remodel took longer than we expected. We spent a month living in my office next door. One day Judy blew up the coffeepot, forgetting to add the water. Our contractor was neglecting us so I spent less and less time counseling in my office and more and more time doubling as handyperson and therapist to our carpenter. One day he got a call from his girlfriend, cursed, and ran out the door, not returning until a week later. Why was I surprised? After all, his truck was adorned with a bumper sticker: "Unless you are a hemorrhoid get off my ass."

Finally, the kitchen was completed. Judy and I were friends again.

❊

In the New Year, about eight months after marriage had become legal in our state, I declared, "We need to get married, Judy, before the state changes its mind." After twenty-five years together, I wanted a wedding celebration with all whom we held dear.

Judy said, "Ok, let's get mood rings and have it on the beach with a luau."

Fortunately, Janice and Lois invited us to their home to see a wedding video of our new friends Marilyn and Paula. They had had a ceremony at their former synagogue in New York City. While marriage was not legal at that time, we were profoundly touched by the sacredness of the service and the support from friends and family. Their Rabbi, Elias Lieberman, a long-time supporter of LGBTQ justice on the Cape, encouraged us along with two other couples. Soon after our gathering, we attended legal ceremonies performed by Rabbi Elias for our friends Marilyn and Paula and Lois and Janice.

Six months later we met with our pastor, Rev. Dr. Ann Michele Rogers-Brigham, to request that she perform our wedding along with our associate pastor, Rev. Gordon Major. Ann Michele was thrilled to officiate at the first same-sex marriage in her church. We had joined the Federated Church of Orleans about a year before that, ten years after I had served as its interim assistant pastor. I had known Ann Michele for many years as a pastoral counselor before she came to Cape Cod. One of the places at which we reconnected was a "Freedom to Marry" clergy event in Boston. Ann Michele was one of the first non-gay clergy to support our rights.

While there was some reservation about the congregation's reaction to our being married there, as well as our own disappointment that the church had voted against being Open and Affirming, we trusted Ann Michele and Gordon and other church members to "make straight the paths of the Lord." I had sometimes fantasized that my marriage would take place at that altar in that church in front of the stained-glass window with the Biblical verse "The Word of our Lord Will Stand Forever." Furthermore, I deeply hoped this church would eventually come to know the gifts of inclusion.

Family and friends were coming from all over the country. We planned a weekend for our celebration, beginning with our Twenty-Fifth Anniversary Cabaret Night on Friday. I painted three large canvases inspired by Toulouse-Lautrec, substituting my own friends' faces for those he had painted. Judy, in her purple hat; Lois, the dancer, became La Goulue; Suzanne, Ellen, and Ed gathered at the Moulin Rouge. At our Cabaret Night we served Greek and Italian food with sangria. Friends brought desserts and hors d'oeuvres. Our friend chanteuse Pavia played accordion and sang in French and Italian. Stan and Loie from New York City created skits and danced. We designed a relationship crossword puzzle. Ellen donned a top hat and cane as our MC. I sang and played Cole Porter's "The Physician" on my guitar for Judy.

Planning the wedding was a challenge since our church didn't hold all the people I wanted to include. Since I had never "formally" come out to my extended family, I struggled with whom to invite. Finally, I reasoned that I would invite mainly people I had kept in touch with and leave enough room for people from the congregation to attend.

There was a cold war going on in my immediate family. Six weeks before the wedding, I told my mother on the phone we would be getting married. Her response was: "Why don't you wait til I die?" I hung up on her. We did not talk for the next month; she also argued with Johnny who came to my defense, and they stopped talking too. This had never happened before in my family. Johnny played the mother role, keeping in touch, asking me about all the arrangements. He, along with Judy's brother Frank, would walk us down the aisle. Johnny volunteered to bring his tuxedo with him that he wore each spring when he attended the Academy Awards. He was very proud to be part of the ceremony; a good friend of his in L.A. told me how my brother had wished that he could have had a permanent partner, and he relished seeing me so happy.

Although Judy would have been OK with mood rings, our rings were designed by our neighbor Ross Coppelman, inscribed with, *il mio cuore e per sempre il vostro* ("my heart is yours always"). I wandered the streets of Chinatown in Boston one morning until I found a Vietnamese woman who designed colorful Chinese jackets. Judy wore a bright red one; I wore gold. Duchy's godmother, Rev. Susan Scribner, baked a luscious five-tier cake, with handmade chocolate poodles dancing among them.

My mother was fearful that her family and friends would find out about the wedding. Her two older sisters, Lena and Rose, in their mid-nineties, had been told already by my outspoken cousin Julie. My aunts called me on the phone, both talking excitedly together. "We love you and Judy. Don't worry about your mother." Oldest sister, Aunty Rosie, said in her usual frank, pointed manner, "Tell your mother, you can fool some of the people some of the time but you can't fool all the people all the time!"

My cousin Julie knew my mother well because my mother had taken care of her and her two brothers after their mother had died suddenly when Julie was a young child. They had all lived in the same three-family home with my grandparents. Julie had the fighting personality of my mother's family; she adored my mother, but she wasn't afraid of her either. She helped me as I labored over which relatives to invite. Julie called my mother and yelled at her: "Be a mother to your daughter!"

Just before the wedding, Aunty Lena called me and said, "Call your mother. Ask her how her leg is." I did, and from there, everything went fine. I think my mother needed to save face and needed me to take the first step. She attended the wedding. Unfortunately, Aunty Lena and Aunty Rose were not healthy enough to make it; both of them died of cancer within a year's time.

The big day arrived. Judy woke up sick with nervousness. I went into high gear, getting to the church early, making sure everything was in order. Betty Kelly, our choir director, played Broadway songs on the piano as people gathered, ending with *West Side Story*'s "Somewhere, A Place for Us." We processed in. Our brothers and Duchy wore matching tuxes with red carnations. Judy entered the sanctuary with Frank, and I followed with Johnny. Duchy was led in by his godmother, Susan. The choir sang:

All things bright and beautiful.
All creatures great and small.
All things wise and wonderful.
The Lord God made them all.

Sister Marie Doyle read Psalm 15 interpreted by Nan Merrill in *Praying the Psalms:*

O Beloved, whom will You invite
into the abode of your Heart?
Who will dwell with You in Love?

Rabbi Rita Sherwin, Judy's college friend, read in Hebrew and English the words of commitment of Ruth and Naomi. Ken, Mary, and Marty from our church choir sang "Simple Song" and "One Hand, One Heart." Our friend Jeanné Brown, an operatic soloist from Georgia, sang "Panis Angelicus" and "O Mio Bambino Caro."

Rev. Gordon Major wrote a special Meditation Poem for us:

What is this strange gladness stirring in us . . .
this impossible dream coming into community?
What was so constant in growing these (twenty five) years,
these two being more one as the beat pulsed,
playing in the delight of knowing and caring
in the fires of a beloved and loving community,
now changes in an eternal promise of one and one.
You rose in us, in song, in solidity, in dance, in healing,
binding us in constellations of uncountable grace,
we continue to name the unknown path as nurture,
    adoption, wholeness,
being alive with one another as we are all in you.
You rose in us in our difference, our brokenness,
our uncompleted selves, our vocations of compassion,
our delight in a variety endlessly the same
challenging us to a deeper courage,
the risk of an eternal covenant.

My friends from Cal Lutheran days, Peg and Reg, now Lutheran co-pastors, gave the Benediction. Betty Kelly played the "Tarantella" for the Recessional. Betsy Bishop came to the church and gave us a gift certificate to Crate and Barrel, for our kitchen.

We said goodbye to Johnny who was staying with us, and we left for a honeymoon in Portland, Maine, with Duchy. My brother didn't look well; he was pale and had lost weight. Looking back, I regret I didn't spend a few more days with him.

FORTY

Letting Go

We never understand how little we need in this
world until we know the loss of it.

—J. M. Barrie, *Margaret Ogilvy*

ON CHRISTMAS EVE, ONLY SIX MONTHS AFTER MY WEDDING, I RUSHED out alone to Los Angeles. Johnny had called me from the ICU just a day after the memorial service for Judy's mother. Her brother Frank and family from Canada was staying with us; Maesine had died a month previously at age eighty-nine—in her sleep—as she had wished. Maesine was raised with her sister Blossom in Detroit. Their father ran the first Chinese-American restaurant in the city before the Great Depression broke the bank and his heart. He died when Maesine was only thirteen. In high school in the 1930s, Maesine met Richard Recknagel, a German-American boy. To the dismay of their families and challenging societal mores against interracial bonding, they married and moved to Cleveland where Richard was a research scientist at Case Western Reserve University. The bulletin at the memorial service had on its cover a large black and white picture of Maesine smiling as she placed an earthenware pot into her kiln to be fired.

Maesine and I loved the arts, meeting in NYC for a Matisse exhibit, hearing jazz in Greenwich Village, and enjoying our trips to Italy. Several months after Richard died, the University of Torino gave him an honorary doctorate for his research on the liver. In spite of Maesine's broken leg, she was determined to accept the award so we all went and were regaled in the medieval pageantry of the University of Torino.

Flying to LA, I worried because I knew that Johnny had not felt well all year. He had lost weight. He had fainting spells and passed out. None of his doctors had uncovered the cause of his condition. Stunned by the heat and feeling desolate as I made my way to the baggage claim, I came face to face with a well-dressed man in a dark pin-striped suit. He handed me his business card. It said Mohammed. I prayed that this was truly a man sent from God as I got into his Lincoln. I told him my brother was in intensive care. He cared. He would offer his Muslim prayers for my brother.

Being alone in Los Angeles at Christmas time and watching the fast decline of my brother's body was hard to digest. I tried to cope when I wasn't at the hospital by visiting the Farmer's Market, having lunch at a Persian café, keeping in touch with my family in Boston, and trying mostly unsuccessfully to round up Johnny's friends in the middle of the holiday. Johnny even gave me some ideas of what to do, not wanting to "ruin my Christmas." The last time we spoke was on Christmas when he had his last meal, a roast beef dinner.

His nurse in the ICU, a Filipino woman, took Johnny's head in her large hands, looked into his eyes, and said, "You have the most beautiful blue eyes. You are more handsome than your sister." Flattery got you everywhere with my brother. I smiled knowing the kindness of her simple gesture.

I grew dependent on the "kindness of strangers." That Christmas morning I took a cab to the Mt. Hollywood Congregational Church. I found the church on the United Church of Christ website listed as an Open and Affirming Church, one I hoped would be supportive of me in this difficult time. I arrived at the church early. Immediately, I introduced myself to the pastor, something I normally wouldn't do. Was I surprised when he told me his parents had lived in Yarmouth and he knew many of my colleagues on the Cape, including Rev. Phil Mitchell? He and his partner drove me after church back to the hospital with a poinsettia for my brother. Two days later he and the associate pastor came to the hospital and prayed at my brother's bedside where he was on life support.

The phone rang at 8 a.m. in my hotel room. It was the Filipino nurse from the ICU. She said softly: "Your brother Johnny is not doing well." I made two phone calls, called the cab, and rushed to the ICU. The nurse came over to tell me that John had died about ten minutes earlier. They did what they could but his heart gave out. She brought me in to see him. He was there yet he wasn't there. I stayed just a few minutes, trying hard to say a goodbye, a prayer, anything. I called his roommate, whom I had not yet met; he wanted to come in so we waited. When he saw him he bent his whole body over and let out a scream.

The day after my brother died, the hospital got the report. I had already suspected the news. The only doctor of several who attended him in the hospital, the only female, a cardiologist, told me the plain truth. He died of late stage AIDS on December 28.

Did he know what was wrong and just covered it up in his many phone conversations with me? Did he even suspect AIDS after he got growths on his back? Was denial and suffering preferable to the truth of coming out to his family? For months afterward I gathered every medical report and visit he ever made, including calling his doctors to ask them point blank if they had asked him about his sexual orientation. They had not. One medical note from an infectious disease specialist whom he had visited claimed that he said he had been tested five years previously for HIV so no test was taken. I wondered if a part of him knew toward the end, but he couldn't let it in. His friend Nathan quipped that he liked to choose doctors for their good looks; I know he gifted them with CDs. Most horrifying was a physician he befriended a couple of years before his death. He had pointed out the doctor's home to me in Laguna Beach, saying he stayed there and took care of his dog. The doctor was later found guilty of giving his patients a saline placebo instead of HIV meds and pocketing the profits!

A circle of love is composed of small acts of caring, sometimes from our loved ones, sometime from strangers. During the time my brother Anthony and I were in LA, we were part of the circle of love of his many friends who created an amazing memorial service for my brother. By word of mouth and email, over seventy people gathered at a United Methodist church in Hollywood. It was the same church I had visited with him a few years previously on Valentine's Day, ballroom dancing with his friends.

This time the church had a huge Christmas tree near the altar and a grand piano. Several of the singers my brother had mentored came and performed along with a guest musician, an eighty-year-old black gentleman. To our amazement he performed the song my brother named his business after, The Hut Sut Song, which Johnny had carried around with him in a box of 45s at the age of three.

The Methodist minister welcomed us and the pastor from Mt. Hollywood Congregational read the eulogy that Anthony and I wrote together. Friends got up and gave moving tributes, laughing and crying. Many expressed gratitude for the ways he reached out to them, often prefacing their remarks with "John was the first person that gave hospitality to me when I first came to the city."

His friends declared, "This is the end of an era." Musicians he nurtured played piano and sang. A large potluck dinner followed. John would have felt at home—hospitality, music, friendship.

For two weeks my brother Anthony and I cleaned out Johnny's apartment. Anthony said, "No one would believe what we did in this short time." I was grateful that Anthony went through his bureaus and clothes. He had a t-shirt collection. Anthony held up various shirts. One said:

Heaven is where the police are British, the chefs Italian, the mechanics German, the lovers French, and it is all organized by the Swiss. Hell is where the police are German, the chefs British, the mechanics French, the lovers Swiss, and it is all organized by the Italians.

Our favorite t-shirt was a print of the Last Supper. The caption underneath read: Who's going to pick up the check? Anthony quipped, "Let's give this to Auntie Portia," our straight-laced Catholic aunt who had adored my brother.

I was shocked at how much stuff was in Johnny's bedroom. All his business stuff, his computer, bank statements, Medicare EOB's, letters from friends from years ago, birthday cards and letters I wrote to him in my twenties. I reorganized it all wishing I could have helped while he was alive, anything that might bring him back and give him a second chance.

Isn't that what I mastered as a pastoral psychotherapist? Helping to reorganize and remodel lives? I thought of Sr. Madeline's words to me at the counseling center in New Bedford: "Your client came in for a touch-up job and you wanted to paint the whole house." Perhaps obsession and compulsion are words of begging and bargaining with God, the opposite of releasing and reframing?

There were many things that Johnny loved that came with me from Los Angeles to Cape Cod. Seventy-five decorative plates of Disney movies from Mary Poppins to Cinderella and Marilyn Monroe. I sold them to a woman named Jean in Vancouver. Tiny music boxes, several hundred CDs, including ones Johnny produced. Just a few albums of the more than thirty boxes of albums were sold or donated in LA. There were stills from old Hollywood movies—*Til the Clouds Roll By, Annie Get Your Gun*—which I sold to a gentleman who drove up from Connecticut. He was of my brother's era, someone appreciating and loving the same Golden Age of film. For the next year, Judy and I enjoyed movie nights with the 100 or more videos I brought back, from *Cat on a Hot Tin Roof* to *Alfred Hitchcock Presents* to *Interrupted Melody*, the story of an opera singer who contacted polio in the 1940s.

Facing decisions when I returned home about all these possessions that defined what mattered to my brother along with the difficult agenda of being his executor and dealing with the thieves in the music business who owed him money, I was inundated with stress.

I was mourning the loss of my brother as spring came and with it the realization that, with our home remodeling, we had lost our English garden. We had snowdrops and crocus in early spring, pale yellow and white iris, and my favorite, red poppies in June. There were glad primroses and the dark foreboding Chinese perilla flowers from Judy's mom, Maesine. How does one prepare for the end of a garden or the loss of a brother? At my clergywomen gathering I shared my dilemma. My friends said they would come to gather the bulbs, the boxwoods, and whatever we wanted them to have.

Rearranging my priorities was not easy. It doesn't just come from the outside in. Instead it is a series of reductions like a sculptor chiseling away pieces of marble to reveal a new image. Digging in the ground, uprooting the crocus buried deep. Reducing my need to do what others expected of me in order to do what really needed to be done. Redeeming the work of my soul and feeding the artist within. Releasing and redeeming—death and rebirth.

FORTY-ONE

Redemption Songs

Blues means what milk does to a baby. Blues is what the
spirit is to the minister. We sing the blues because our hearts
have been hurt, our souls have been disturbed.

—Alberta Hunter, from *American Singers: Twenty-Seven Portraits in Song,*
by Whitney Balliett

AFTER JOHNNY DIED THAT CHRISTMAS, I RETURNED HOME IN THE NEW Year to receive eleven boxes of books. *Walking with Grief: A Healing Journey* began as a collaborative project with Rev. Nanette Geertz. I had companioned Nan as she uncovered a call to the ordained ministry. Her life had already expressed itself beautifully as a ministry with children in the churches her husband, Bill, had pastored. One day she took a walk nearby toward the marshes and the sea. Returning, she handed me two sheets of paper and said softly in her gentle yet playful way, "During my walk I realized you might find a way to illustrate this."

Her hand-written poem begins, "My daughter died. She was only nineteen. I am very sad. I go for walks in the winter, dusk . . . where has my Jennifer gone?"

Nan desired to show her children at church in simple verse how one heals after losing a loved one.

"Yes," I replied, touched by the fragility of her loss and all our griefs that I could only bear to approach in baby steps.

"I will make a painting for each verse. Give me time to ponder before I raise my brush."

I never met Nan's daughter, but Nan gave me a school photo that I kept on my easel. The last painting, titled *Jennifer*, is like an icon, a holy interpretation of Jennifer's spirit, which, like the love of God, is never separated from all that she is and will be.

Six months later, Nan walked upstairs to my studio to see my progress. My vision of Jennifer's spirit as an evolving presence in her mother's life brought solace to Nan. The poem and paintings became a healing service, allowing parishioners at her church to walk by each picture and verse as one might do at Stations of the Cross.

Nan fulfilled her dream of becoming a Protestant minister like her husband and father. I had the privilege to witness and guide her emerging call just as Jim had done for me years ago in spiritual direction. Her new call blossomed only for a few short years before the cough that led to her reoccurrence of breast cancer. She died in early March, the week of my birthday. I will always remember the last time we visited. Together we rode the little bus in Heritage Gardens in Sandwich, and we walked, she with her cane, the labyrinth under an enormous wise old tree trunk, its branches bending and shaping a path. A life shared, a labyrinth, not a maze of confusion but a way to a God that can make a way when there is no way, no there there, only beauty and respite for our tired souls.

Walking with Grief, published by Healthsigns, became a ministry of its own, a healing balm of promise and hope.

"I will do a new art series modeled after classic female jazz vocalists!"

My jazz/blues epiphany began as a teenager in Filene's Basement where I purchased my first Billie Holliday album for 49 cents. The deep purple jacket with the Verve label showed a profile of a woman's head with a gardenia. Her rich voice transformed melancholy into beauty as she sang "You Go to My Head" and "Good Morning Heartache," ending with her haunting "Strange Fruit." This album secured my entryway to blues; angst and pent-up emotions swirled through my body then pushed out like a trombone as I lay on the couch in my solitude in my family's finished basement. Billie gave me the sounds of emotions I could neither explain nor express.

In Manhattan I drank in the living presence of magnificent jazz vocalists. At the Blue Note in Greenwich Village, Carmen McRae's seductive presence and beautiful phrasing spoke intimately to me. Miss Lena Horne was triumphant in her one-woman show as she had come into her own—proud, brilliant, and beautiful.

Blues singer Alberta Hunter uplifted me with her playfulness and joy. She made a comeback at age eighty-two at the Cookery in Greenwich Village after working many years as a nurse. I brought Judy to hear her in our courtship days. When we got to the Cookery, there was a long waiting line. The bouncer stopped us, saying they were full. "You have to let us in. We came all the way from Cape Cod." I insisted and implored, impressing and delighting my new love as we were ushered into the Cookery with its vinyl booths and black-and-white checkered floor. Alberta came over to our table and signed with a flourish, "All my best, to Anne and Judy." Hands on her hips, she proclaimed: "I'm having a good time."

My jazz series included paintings of twelve women: Alberta Hunter, Lena Horne, Billie Holiday, Rosemary Clooney, Ella Fitzgerald, Shirley Horn, Sarah Vaughan, Cleo Laine, Carmen McRae, Anita O'Day, Ethel Waters, and Dinah Washington. When I realized that people had little idea of the lives and the struggles of these ladies of jazz, I read about their lives and wrote summaries to post next to the paintings on exhibit.

Creativity and Madness, an art and psychology conference, took me to Barcelona to give a presentation to psychiatrists on Billie Holiday, Alberta Hunter, and Rosie Clooney. I described it this way: "We will explore the concept of authenticity in the lives and music of Billie Holiday, Alberta Hunter, and Rosemary Clooney. These artists lived and worked through most decades of the twentieth century. They battled addiction, failed marriages, the sexism and racism of Hollywood, the music industry, and American culture. The depth of their emotional expression has much to teach us and our clients about honesty, authenticity, and resilience."

❋

The phone rang. It was my mother.

"I just want to thank you and your brother for all you have done for me. I can't get over it. When I die I will pray for you. I am going to hang up before I start crying."

My brother got the same call that night. "It only took ninety-eight years," he quipped.

I knew the love was there. I experienced its depth when she was ninety-one, grieving not so openly as she did for my dad but as a mother who remembered her sweet blonde, blue-eyed kid in the sailor suit. I wondered if she regretted her inability to accept John fully, the unspoken ways that kept him from caring for himself. My mother matured as good wine does, deepening her ability to love, to give thanks for "every day that I get out of bed and put my feet on the floor," and to nurture relationships among her helpers and friends. It was as if a new family grew around her.

My mother celebrated her 100th birthday in 2014. Family and friends, including the doctor she worked for in the lab at Harvard, toasted her. I invited my jazz musician friends to play and sing. She sat like a queen in an arm chair with headphones (a poor man's hearing aid), her white hair that she finally stopped coloring, and an orchid corsage from Anthony. Lines of people greeted her, and she took her time with each, asking by name after the children's children. Who could remember? But she did. Happily opening her many gifts. What do you get someone at 100? Something fun, something beautiful. A white pillow with the word "Joy" embroidered in silver for her living room couch.

Her prophecy came true: "I am going to die in my own bed." Shy of her 102nd birthday, she had been through enough rehab, surviving a fall down the basement stairs one year and a trapped kidney stone the next. Judy and I and Donna, who cooked Italian food for her on Saturdays, were seated around her kitchen table, drinking white wine and sharing stories. When Donna went to kiss her goodbye, she had left this world.

You shouldn't be grieved at this, but have joy and gladness in it, considering
that I am leaving a place of great suffering and going to rest in the
pacific sea, God eternal, to be united to my most sweet bridegroom. I
promise you that I will be more perfectly with you, and will be able
to help you more there than I have been able to do here, as I will be
delivered from darkness and united with the true and eternal light.

—St. Catherine of Siena, words spoken on her deathbed in 1380 as her followers wept; from *The Road to Siena: The Essential Biography of St. Catherine*, by Edmund Gardner

FORTY-TWO

Stalking the Gaps at Low Tide

The gaps are the thing. The gaps are the spirit's one home . . . Go
up into the gaps. If you can find them; they shift and vanish too.
Stalk the gaps. Squeak into a gap in the soil, turn, and unlock—
more than a maple—a universe. This is how you spend this
afternoon, and tomorrow morning, and tomorrow afternoon.

—Annie Dillard, *Pilgrim at Tinker Creek*

Life is a bigger mystery than we can grasp. We can either spend our days running away from life or running toward life. I have crossed many bridges in my life and I have tried to make bridges.

In the fall of 2019, I made a pilgrimage to civil rights sites in the south. As I stood at the foot of the Edmund Pettus Bridge, I recalled how my colleagues had made "good trouble" to be faithful to their calls. Now I have eyes to see and ears to hear how God still speaks, still calls for our witness. Often I saw alternatives to the usual approach, so I tried them out; choosing two or three things instead of just one. I attended two colleges: one Protestant on the west coast; the other Catholic on the east coast. And three seminaries. Why? I was curious, hungry to learn, seeking balance. Moreover, I desired to experience life from the other side, to stalk the gaps, to come alive.

The Cape is a place for contemplation and, over time, people like me who come from the city learn to live a bit more unobtrusively, appreciative of the natural beauty of sea and shore, the fragility of our environment, and its dependence on us as caretakers.

We tell stories to one another about deeds well done. We discuss unmet needs and ways to make a difference. We learn to relish the unique characters who make their home here. One day we realize we may become a character too. We crisscross paths forming a creative web of generativity.

There are many hidden places on Cape Cod only reached by jeep or boat. Late one afternoon I felt exquisitely fortunate to spend it on the Dennis flats at low tide with Judy and Duchy. We watched as the tide receded. Where did it go? It became safe to drive across to the edge of the new shore and watch the sun set as the sky painted its colors. Our host sat us on beach chairs while she prepared a gourmet seafood meal. Looking to the left, we saw the crescent moon. My little dog ran for joy, being free of leashes and walls. I followed, allowing my legs to run after him.

In the darkness of ocean depths and the sea's ceaseless waves, in the glistening of a creature's eyes and the dark life-blood that ever flows . . . In every shining of the world's inwardness and the warmth that moves my everliving soul your glory glows, O God.

—John Philip Newell, *Sounds of the Eternal: A Celtic Psalter*

I am called to the spaces, the gaps, the new frontier in church and world. Over the past few years, through Dr. Margaret Benefiel's Soul of Leadership retreats and Sr. Joan Chittister's *Monasteries of the Heart,* a new way has emerged to gather people for spiritual and artistic expression.

A call to the gaps may prove risky or difficult, not as safe as staying on dry land. Like Alice in Wonderland, I still fall into holes. These holes, these gaps are not like the story of the person who keeps falling into the same hole over and over. Instead, I fall into spaces of wonder and amazement.

What if?

Author's Notes about Sources by Page Number

13   Emily Dickinson, "I Never Saw a Moor"

21   Soren Kierkegaard, from *The Concept of Anxiety*

30   Attributed to Michelangelo.

40   Anna Akhmatova, exact source unknown

40   Giuseppe Verdi, from the opera *Attila*

40   Dante Alighieri, Canto XXVI

43   Karl Menninger, "Take Your Choice," *This Week's Magazine*, Oct., 1949

53   William Wordsworth, "Ode on Intimations of Immortality from Recollections of Early Childhood"

59   Zora Neale Hurston, *Their Eyes Were Watching God*. J. B. Lippincott, 1937.

63   Joanna Clapps Herman, *The Anarchist Bastard: Growing Up Italian in America*. Albany: SUNY Press, 2011. [www.joanna-clappsherman.com]

66   Elie Wiesel, *Memoirs: All Rivers Run to the Sea*. New York: Knopf, 1995.

68   Rubáiyát of Omar Khayyám (Edward Fitzgerald)

73   Marion Woodman, *Addiction to Perfection*, 1982

79   Rev. Granger Westberg

82   Catherine Doherty, Madonna House Staff Letter #140

87   Derek Walcott, "Odd Job: A Bull Terrier"

91   Thomas Merton, Faith and Violence, 1968

93   The Diary of Anaïs Nin, 1944–1947

99   Carter Heyward, *Touching Our Strength: The Erotic as Power and the Love of God*. New York: Harper & Row, 1989.

101   Simone Weil, *Waiting for God*, 1950

105   Katie Geneva Cannon

106   Carter Heyward, *Touching Our Strength*

108   Sr. Marjorie Tuite, OP, from a talk given in Los Angeles, 1986

118   Marion Woodman, *Coming Home to Myself*, 1998

120   Willa Cather, *The Song of the Lark*, 1915

129   Deacon Pat Guerrini, from a talk given at the author's ordination

135   Kip Tiernan, *Urban Meditations*

157   Henri Nouwen, talk given at Harvard Divinity School

172   Vincent van Gogh from a letter to his brother, Theo van Gogh, May 14, 1882.

174   James Baldwin, *New York Times Book Review*, January 14, 1962

181   Katherine Mansfield, compiled by John Middleton Murry, *The Journal of Katherine Mansfield*, 1927

181   Attributed to William James

186   J. M. Barrie, *Margaret Ogilvy*, 1896

190   Alberta Hunter, from *American Singers: Twenty-Seven Portraits in Song*, by Whitney Balliett, 1979

193   St. Catherine of Siena, words spoken on her deathbed in 1380 as her followers wept; from *The Road to Siena: The Essential Biography of St. Catherine*, by Edmund Gardner, 2009

193   Annie Dillard, *Pilgrim at Tinker Creek*, 1974

194   John Philip Newell, *Sounds of the Eternal: A Celtic Psalter*, 2002

About the Author

ANNE M. IERARDI is an expressive artist and writer. Creative expression, whether visual art, writing, or music, defines Anne's identity and search for wholeness and the Holy. She cofounded Healthsigns Center, a sanctuary for counseling, contemplative worship, and community gatherings. Healthsigns published *Walking with Grief: A Healing Journey* with her impressionistic paintings. She is a member of the Authors Guild, the Cape Cod Writers Center, and the International Women Writer's Guild. Born in Boston to a large extended Italian-American family, she traveled from Boston to California to Italy and finally to Cape Cod to nurture her passion for art and writing. In her early thirties she experienced a faith epiphany leading to seminary at the Episcopal Divinity School (M.Div.) and to a doctoral program (D.Min.) at Boston University, writing her thesis on women's faith development. Dr. Ierardi practiced for many years as a pastoral psychotherapist. Rev. Dr. Ierardi is an ordained minister in the American Baptist and United Church of Christ traditions, serving people of all backgrounds. With her wife, Dr. Judy Recknagel, she developed wholistic approaches to the healing arts and astrology. They were honored for their leadership of the Cape Cod Coalition of Welcoming Congregations and are listed in the *National Women's Hall of Fame Book of Lives & Legacies*. You can view her art, blogs, and writings at www.anneierardi.com.